APRIL 22, 1970—EARTH DAY

Nearly 20 million people participated. It was the largest, cleanest, most peaceful demonstration in America's history. But don't call it a success. Because the problems are still with us. Pollution. Overpopulation. Overkill. Slums. Racism. Wasted resources. Planned obsolescence. A widening war.

On April 22, a generation dedicated itself to reclaiming the planet. A new kind of movement was born—a bizarre alliance that spans the ideological spectrum from campus militants to middle Americans. Its aim: to reverse our rush toward extinction. If the environmental movement succeeds it will profoundly change corporations, government and the way each of us lives. But it faces obstacles that are political as well as technical. And the battle lines are already being drawn. In this book, edited by the national coordinators of Earth Day, more than fifty of the people who spoke on April 22 map the next decade's most urgent, and perhaps most bitter, issues—conflicts which will be decided in legislatures, in courts, in hearings, in stockholders' meetings, and in the streets.

EARTH DAY—THE BEGINNING

Compiled and edited by the National Staff of
Environmental Action

Each of the contributors to this book has donated his selection to Environmental Action for inclusion in this book. Royalties from the sale of the book will be used by Environmental Action to continue its work.

AN ARNO PRESS/NEW YORK TIMES BOOK

Earth Day—The Beginning

A Guide for Survival

Compiled and edited by the National Staff of environmental action

A NATIONAL GENERAL COMPANY

EARTH DAY—THE BEGINNING
A Bantam Book / published May 1970

ACKNOWLEDGMENTS

"The Beginning," by Denis A. Hayes. Copyright © 1970 by Denis A. Hayes.

"The Future Is Circular," by Alan Gussow. Copyright © 1970 by Alan Gussow.

"Tragedy of the Commons," by Garrett Hardin. Copyright © 1970 by Garrett Hardin.

"Nixon's the One," by Kurt Vonnegut, Jr. Copyright © 1970 by Kurt Vonnegut, Jr.

"Imperialism," by Joseph Shapiro. Copyright © 1970 by Joseph Shapiro.

"Roots of Crisis," by Barbara Reid. Copyright © 1970 by Barbara J. Reid.

"Two-ton Gadgets," by Walter P. Reuther. Copyright © 1970 by Estate of Walter P. Reuther.

"Sue the Bastards," by Victor J. Yannacone, Jr. Copyright © 1970 by Victor John Yannacone, Jr.

"Five Acres," by Eugene P. Odum. Copyright © 1970 by Eugene P. Odum.

"La Raza," by Arturo Sandoval. Copyright © 1970 by Arturo Sandoval.

For information address: Arno Press, Inc.,
330 Madison Avenue, New York, N.Y. 10017.

Published simultaneously in the United States and Canada

Bantam Books are published by Bantam Books, Inc., a National General company. Its trade-mark, consisting of the words "Bantam Books" and the portrayal of a bantam, is registered in the United States Patent Office and in other countries. Marca Registrada. Bantam Books, Inc., 666 Fifth Avenue, New York, N.Y. 10019.

PRINTED IN THE UNITED STATES OF AMERICA

To the tree
from which this book is made

A WORD ABOUT THE BOOK

In organizing for Earth Day, Environmental Action served as the national coordinating office for local groups on 2,000 campuses, in 2,000 communities and in 10,000 high schools throughout the country. We provided information on environmental problems and what local groups were doing about them. And, where we could, we helped people to organize effective local organizations. Now that Earth Day is over, their role—and ours—has changed. Groups whose Earth Day programs were mostly talk are mapping strategies for action. And groups whose action so far has consisted mostly of trash pick-ups are becoming convinced that preserving life on this planet will take more than a few individuals' doing their civic duty.

Anyone who is serious about saving the environment must prepare for a long and difficult fight, as will be clear from the speeches collected here. That is why we have compiled them. Except where otherwise instructed by a contributor, we have felt free to take excerpts which make a unique point, although it may not have been the major thrust of the speech.

Some of these selections indicate solutions; some are part of the problem. All of them, we hope, contribute to an understanding of just how much must be done.

Environmental Action
DENIS HAYES, National Coordinator

Steve Cotton
Andrew Garling
Steve Haft
Bryce Hamilton
Mike Harris
Linda Katz
Sam Love

Phil Michael
Judy Moody
Sally Morrill
Barbara Reid
Arturo Sandoval
Janet Schaeffer
Susan Winslow

WALTER P. REUTHER 1907–1970

We would like to pay tribute to Walter Reuther, a friend and ally in the movement for peace, justice, and a livable environment. We admired his courage and his foresight, and we are deeply grateful for the help he gave us.

ACKNOWLEDGMENTS

A lot of people have come to our aid during one crisis or another since we began organizing in January. Those to whom we are indebted include Linda Billings, Kent Conrad, Charles Creasey, Paul Ehrlich, Sydney Howe, Joe, Harold Jordahl, Marianna Kaufman, Vic Kley, Daniel Lufkin, Olga Madar, Anthony Mazzochi, Representative Paul McCloskey, Moose, Sally Morrill, Senator Gaylord Nelson, Glenn Paulson, Douglas Scott, Bernie Trilling, Barbara Wagner, Frank Wallick and John Yolton.

For their part in the Earth Day be-in at the Washington Monument, we'd like to thank the Chambers Brothers; Charlie, Bev, Cousin Julius and Chester; Pete Seeger and his troupe; Mical Whitaker and his troupe; Phil Ochs; Steve Nicholas; Claude Jones; Oliver and Big Bill; The Hog and Lois; Dick Holler and Zach; Love Cry Want; Elliot Ryan; Gigi & Patti; Baze Water; Babe; Tractor; Lufian Fire; Bill Drennen; Bob Waldrop; the kid who came all the way from Florida; Al Dotoli; Roger Priest; Linda Cusack; I. F. Stone; the Reverend Channing Phillips; Rennie Davis; Joe Onek; Senator Edmund Muskie; Ray Swenson and the CBS crew; Tim Pace; Lights By Us; Yorktown Power & Light; Chuck Levin and the Washington Musical Center; the guy who stole the piano; and, of course, Debbie.

Julie Maxey and Pat Segnan spent a month

researching and editing speeches in a frenetic office, serenely pulling the whole thing together. Julie provided invaluable editorial assistance, Pat production know-how. They have both been beautiful beyond all telling.

We also greatly appreciate the editorial help we received from Jack Shepherd, who advised us at the start and at crucial points along the way; his wife Kathy; and Dave Maxey. We thank the aides who somehow got the speeches from their bosses to us in time to meet our deadline, and the people at campuses throughout the country who taped programs for us.

And we are especially grateful to the contributors who generously donated their speeches for use in this book.

STEVE COTTON
Editor

Washington, D.C.
May, 1970

CONTENTS

DENIS HAYES

The Beginning

Sylvan Theater, Washington, D.C., April 22

I suspect that the politicians and businessmen who are jumping on the environmental bandwagon don't have the slightest idea what they are getting into. They are talking about filters on smokestacks while we are challenging corporate irresponsibility. They are bursting with pride about plans for totally inadequate municipal sewage treatment plants; we are challenging the ethics of a society that, with only 6 percent of the world's population, accounts for more than half of the world's annual consumption of raw materials.

Our country is stealing from poorer nations and from generations yet unborn. We seem to have a reverse King Midas touch. Everything we touch turns to garbage—142 tons of smoke, 7 million junked cars, 30 million tons of paper, 28 billion bottles, 48 billion cans each year. We waste riches in planned obsolescence and invest the overwhelming bulk of our national budget in ABMs and MIRVs and other means of death. Russia can destroy every American twelve times; America can destroy every Russian forty times. I guess that is supposed to mean that we are ahead.

We're spending insanely large sums on military hardware instead of eliminating hunger and poverty. We squander our resources on moon dust while people live in wretched housing. We still waste lives and money on a war that we should never have entered and should get out of immediately.

We have made Vietnam an ecological catastrophe. Vietnam was once capable of producing a marketable surplus of grain. Now America must feed her. American bombs have pockmarked Vietnam with more than 2.6 million craters a year, some of them thirty feet deep. We spent $73 million on defoliation in Vietnam last year alone, much of it on 2,4,5–T, a herbicide we've now found causes birth defects. We dumped defoliants on Vietnam at the rate of 10,000 pounds a month, and in the last fiscal year alone we blackened 6,600 square miles. We cannot pretend to be concerned with the environment of this or any other country as long as we continue the war in Vietnam or wage war in Cambodia, Laos, or anywhere else.

But even if that war were over tomorrow, we would still be killing this planet. We are systematically destroying our land, our streams, and our seas. We foul our air, deaden our senses, and pollute our bodies. And it's getting worse.

America's political and business institutions don't seem yet to have realized that some of us want to live in this country thirty years from now. They had better come to recognize it soon. We don't have very much time. We cannot afford to give them very much time.

When it comes to salvaging the environment, the individual is almost powerless. You can pick up litter, and if you're diligent, you may be able to find some returnable bottles. But you are forced to breathe the lung-corroding poison which companies spew into the air. You cannot buy electricity from a power company which does not pollute. You cannot find products in biodegradable packages. You cannot even look to the manufacturer for reliable information on the ecological effects of a product.

You simply can't live an ecologically sound life in America. That is not one of the options open to you. Go shopping and you find dozens of laundry products; it seems like a tremendous array unless you know that most are made by three companies, and the differences in cleaning power are almost negligible. If you really want to be ecologically sound, you won't buy any detergents—just some old-fashioned laundry soap and a bit of soda. But there's nothing on those packages to tell you the phosphate content, and there's nothing in the supermarket to tell you, only meaningless advertising that keeps dunning you.

We are learning. In response, industry has turned the environmental problem over to its public relations men. We've been deluged with full-page ads about pollution problems and what's being done about them. It would appear from most of them that things are fine and will soon be perfect. But the people of America are still coughing. And our eyes are running, and our lungs are blackening, and our property is corroding, and we're getting angry. We're getting angry at half-truths, angry at semitruths, and angry at outright lies.

We are tired of being told that we are to blame for corporate depredations. Political and business leaders once hoped that they could turn the environmental movement into a massive antilitter campaign. They have failed. We have learned not to place our faith in regulatory agencies that are supposed to act in the public interest. We have learned not to believe the advertising that sells us presidents the way it sells us useless products.

We will not appeal any more to the conscience of institutions because institutions have no conscience. If we want them to do what is right, we must make them do what is right. We will use proxy fights, lawsuits, demonstrations, research, boycotts, ballots—whatever it takes. This may be our last chance. If environment is a fad, it's going to be our last fad.

Things as we know them are falling apart. There is an unease across this country today. People know that something is wrong. The war is part of it, but most critics of the war have, from the beginning, known that the war is only a symptom of something much deeper. Poor people have long known what is wrong. Now the alley garbage, the crowding and the unhappiness and the crime have spread beyond the ghetto and a whole society is coming to realize that it must drastically change course.

We are building a movement, a movement with a broad base, a movement which transcends traditional political boundaries. It is a movement that values people more than technology, people more than political boundaries and political ideologies, people more than profit. It will be a difficult fight. Earth Day is the beginning.

Denis Hayes is national coordinator of Environmental Action.

EARTH DAY—
THE BEGINNING

PART I

EARTH'S LAST STAND

Aboard one of the U.S. Navy's deep submersible craft, fifty miles off the coast of San Diego, and 2,450 feet down, Admiral R. J. Galanson, chief of naval materials, peered through the portholes to view the wonders of the undersea world which perhaps no other man had ever seen. The first thing he spotted, only two feet away on the ocean floor, was an empty beer can.

—State Senator Leslie Robinson
Kearney State College
Kearney, Nebr.
April 22

ALAN GUSSOW

The Future Is Circular

Bryant Park, New York City, April 22

Valéry once wrote, "The main trouble with the world today is that the future is not what it used to be." When I was a kid growing up we had a war. Many people were killed and many others were made unhappy. But that war, World War II, had a beginning and it did have an end—or at least we thought it did. Our sense of the future then also had clear beginnings and endings. First school, then college, then the army, then a job ("Does it offer good retirement benefits?" graduates used to ask)—this was the predictable sequence. One could plan. We had shortages—perhaps it was tough getting a new car right after the war—but no one ever thought in terms of the big problems. Pollution hadn't been invented, and if anyone suggested we might be tampering with "nonrenewable resources" he would have been looked at like some sort of a nut. Population problems were unknown. Our only problems were personal—getting a job, making money, finding a girl to marry, and so forth. The future was like our sense of the Earth—long, flat, endless. After reaching each goal, we would advance on to the next. Life was a long road.

The future today isn't what it used to be. We live now in a world with two futures, both new and both coexistent. There is the short future, tomorrow, or maybe even tonight. If we can get through the day, that's enough. Who can really think about a distant future when, for example, life in a ghetto hits some of us every day with the question of simple survival. So one view of the future is that no real future exists.

Then there is another view of the future which in a sense is what Earth Day is all about. This view suggests calamity lies ahead if we don't stop doing some of the things we seem to be insistently doing, things like polluting the air, destroying our rivers, killing our oceans, and jamming our cities. Such a view of the future is circular like the whole Earth. A circular future means that we cannot escape from whatever it is that we do here and now. Life is not linear, it is round. If we pollute the Earth and others do the same, the pollution will come up over the horizon one day and destroy us. . . .

ALAN GUSSOW is an artist and conservationist.

KENNETH E. F. WATT

Whole Earth

Swarthmore College, Swarthmore, Pa., April 19

About three years ago it became obvious that a large number of problems were attributable to a rapidly increasing population. . . . I have developed an extremely strong view in the course of this period . . . as to what the central issues are. They are not at all what they are generally believed to be.

The Now Generation

There are actually several different interlocking problems that have to do with the decision-making processes of of all of us. One of the most basic of these is that modern technological man, whether you find him in Germany, Japan, United States, Britain, or elsewhere, is extraordinarily now-oriented. Let me give you an example. Many thousands of years before the birth of Christ you all know that three very large pyramids were built in Egypt. Each of these pyramids took twenty years to build, and by the time they went to the second and third pyramid, everybody knew they took twenty years to build. This happened at a time when the average person lived only thirty-five years. So, three successive projects were undertaken, each of which took about half the lifetime of an average person. By the time the Middle Ages came, the attitude of the people and culture toward time had changed to the point where the great cathedral of Notre Dame in Paris took ninety years to build when the average Parisian lived only forty-five years. Now people were prepared to undertake a project that took just twice the lifetime of an average person—that is, four times as long relative to a person's lifetime as the pyramids of Egypt. In modern times, the longest project that man has been prepared to undertake is the exploration of the moon, which took twelve years from conception to completion at a time when most people live six times that long. So, in contradistinction to the Middle Ages, when people were prepared to spend two adult lifetimes on a project, we are now prepared to spend only one-sixth of an adult lifetime on a project.

Now, counterarguments can be raised to this line of reasoning. People say, well, they were building pyramids and cathedrals for their own mortal souls. The fact is that in many other areas of activity utterly untouched by religious considerations, people in the past have been prepared to work on very long projects. Interestingly enough, if you want very long runs of data in many fields of science you find that they are obtainable for the time up to 1940, but not for the time after 1940. The fact is, we have become a culture which is rather unique in human history, in that we live in the present and don't think much about the past and don't think much about the future. This is probably the most now-oriented culture that has ever lived.

This leads us to a number of other problems. One is that we tend constantly to overestimate the value of present benefits relative to future benefits. . . . Let me give you one interesting example of this. One of the things that our computer studies have revealed is that most of the problems about which our politicians are currently most exercised—crime and violence in the streets, adequate tax support for higher education, and so on—are simply due to the fact that our society is growing too fast. . . . As the growth rate increases, you have more young people, in education-tax consuming ages [and relatively fewer] older people in education-tax producing ages. So there is a relationship between the tax burden per taxpayer and the rate of population growth, something that has been given very little attention. Further, the incidence of crime and violence per person is maximal between the ages of about sixteen and twenty-four. Any increase in population growth means that for that reason alone there will be an increase in the incidence of crime and violence.

Now, what is not generally known, even among those people who are familiar with this principle, is the amazing sensitivity of the tax burden to very small changes in the rate of population increase. For example, if the rate of population increase goes up from no increase to just 1 percent per annum, this means that the tax burden per taxpayer is 25 percent higher than it would have been if the population was not growing. If the population growth rate goes up from zero population growth to 3 percent per annum, the tax burden per taxpayer for education taxes alone is about three times what it would be in a stable population. But if a population is growing 10 percent per annum, then the tax burden per taxpayer is between ten and eleven times what it would be in a stable population. There *have* been times and places in the United States since the Second World War where the population was actually growing 10 percent per annum, and now everybody is sitting around with egg and custard on his face.

I am wondering how we got into this strange predicament where we don't seem to be able to afford our educational systems. There is a very simple explanation. We became so now-oriented that we became blinded by all the benefits of population growth so that we could not see the immense cost. Now the chickens are coming home to roost—the crime and violence and all the difficulties surrounding the payment for educational institutions, and all the rioting because the students feel they don't have enough services, and so on. There is a very simple explanation. We are growing too fast. We are not prepared to face up to the fact that in a society which has a high and rapidly rising standard of living, you simply can't have any population growth. The tax system won't meet the cost.

Fossil-Fuel Subsidy

Now, another problem that's related to this notion that our society is very now-oriented is our failure to look ahead far enough to even *think* about the possibilities that there might be limits on anything. This is leading to some absolutely unimaginable disasters. Let me give a case in point. Let's take energy and the dependence of our whole pattern of civilization on energy. Not only do we have a very high rate of consumption of fossil fuel in the United States, but that rate of consumption is rising rapidly, here and elsewhere, relative to the total amount of fossil fuel that we have.

The rate of consumption of crude oil in the world is going up 6.9 percent per annum. There literally isn't a mechanism in sight that will make this rate ease off. In 1965, the world burned 11 billion barrels. A 6.9 percent per annum rate of increase in crude-oil consumption and production means that you have a doubling time of ten years. That means that in 1975 we will be burning up 22 billion barrels of crude oil. By 1985, 44; by 1995, 88; and by the year 2000, 123 billion barrels of crude oil a year. . . . By the year 2000, if present trends continue, we will be using up crude oil at such a high rate, without regard to pollution or anything else, that there simply won't be any more crude oil. You'll drive up to the pump and say, "Fill 'er up, buddy," and he'll say, "I am very sorry, there isn't any." We simply haven't thought about the fact that this high and rapidly rising rate of increase means that someday we run out. The entertaining thing is that we actually have no excuse for this. We have had the fantastically illuminating experience of seeing pictures of our planet from outer space, showing that it is a small, lonely ball in empty space. Now, that should dispel any notion that we live on an infinite planet or that we have a flat Earth. We in fact live on a small round ball that logic dictates must have limited resources, yet we are proceeding to behave as if there were absolutely infinite resources. There aren't.

It is really frightening that we have failed to grasp the significance of the fact that our whole society was switching from resources that are dependent upon incoming solar radiation every year to resources called stock resources. These are resources that have been built up over a period of time because of past activity of the sun, but which will run out someday. . . .

Any farmer or rancher or wildlife manager knows that a given acreage of range has a certain carrying capacity for animals. He also knows that he can increase that carrying capacity by adding hay or grain. One of the ultimate extensions of this is in the finishing feedlot for cattle, where very large numbers of cattle are kept in a small enclosed space to be finished off just before going to market, and a tremendous mass of hay and grain is moved into this space. What has happened is that the carrying capacity of the environment for cattle, the ability of a certain amount of acreage to support livestock, has been built up by an energy subsidy. . . . Those of you who are fish fanciers will be familiar with the same concept in the form of an aquarium. You can increase the number of fish you can support in an aquarium simply by increasing the fish food. Now, what we have completely overlooked is that if you remove that added food, then suddenly the population must go down. There will be mass mortality. In effect, our planet is an aquarium for a given acreage of rangeland, and we have been increasing the energy subsidy since about 1820 by adding a fossil-fuel subsidy to our agricultural systems. To give you an idea of how massive an impact this has had, we will consider just one thing that we have done that way. Between 1950 and the present, a final 11 million horses have been taken out of American agriculture and replaced by tractors powered by crude oil. Since it takes very roughly four times the acreage to support one horse as a person, this means that we have been able to add 44 million people to the American population from 1950 to the present for that one cause alone, because of a fossil-fuel energy subsidy.

The fact is that we have been making this fossil-fuel energy subsidy through our whole agricultural system in many, many different ways. For instance, we use an immense amount of fossil fuel to get fertilizer out of the ground, manufacture commercial fertilizer, bag it, get it into the trucks, truck it long distances to farms where it is applied, and power the tractors which apply it.

Furthermore, the entire world system of agriculture is converting to this kind of practice, so that, for instance, in northwestern India we're converting very rapidly from a man-bullock system to a man–tractor–crude-oil system. But I just told you we're going to be out of crude oil about the year 2000 or shortly thereafter. What happens then?

Alternative Fuel Sources

You'll all say, "Well, no problem." In fact, this is what all the technological optimists say—no problem whatsoever—we're going to be saved by atomic energy. Really? There are three ways you can get energy from the atom. You can make industrial use of the controlled fission action in what is called the "burner" or "converter" reactor, which takes the material in uranium ores and simply burns it up as if it were coal or crude oil. Once burned, it's gone forever. That's what we're doing now. All the world's cheap uranium ores are being used up that way, remarkably quickly. And that won't last; that won't last any longer than crude oil or coal.

. . . The second possibility is to use "breeder" reactors, which make use of the controlled fission process to get a large amount of fissionable material out of the energy-producing process as you use up fissionable material. So essentially you have a self-sustaining system. However, we don't have a breeder reactor working yet.

The third possibility is to use a controlled fusion process to make use of the reaction that goes on in the sun; and this, indeed, would give us an energy source that would keep us going forever. There's only one problem. If you talk to many of the leading physicists or geologists or other scientists in the country who are knowledgeable about atomic energy, they will simply tell you right out that the people working on the breeder reaction, or the third kind —the controlled fusion reaction—have been telling us now for many, many years that just wait another twenty years and we'll have it for you. They are essentially telling us that now. There are beginning to be very serious problems raised as to whether or not we'll ever get these things.

This leads to a remarkable conclusion: Mankind is embarked on an absolutely immense gamble. We are letting the population build up and up and up, by increasing the carrying capacity of the Earth for people, using a crude-oil energy subsidy, on the assumption that there's no inherent danger in this because when the need arises we'll be able to get ultimate sources of energy. Yet the only ultimate source of energy that modern science sees as being even being possible in principle we have been working on for many years and we don't have.

Maybe we will get the breeder reaction, and maybe we will get the controlled fusion reaction; but I haven't found a scientist in the United States who will say there is a 100 percent certainty that that will occur. In other words, we're gambling for the life of mankind, and we're gambling for very high stakes in a situation where we aren't certain that we can pull off the gamble. Wouldn't it be more prudent to show for sure that we could get the fast breeder reaction going or the controlled fusion reaction, and then let the population build up—if, indeed, we decide we want to let it build up in the face of other evidence indicating that a buildup would be deleterious.

. . . The world can probably support between one and four billion people at the absolute outside without a fossil-fuel energy subsidy. My guess is that number is closer to one billion. By the time we run out of this fossil fuel energy subsidy, there will be 10 to 20 billion people in the world. Now, suppose we run out of fossil fuel and it turns out we don't have nuclear energy. What's going to happen during the period when we drop very suddenly, in about three years, from between 10 and 20 billion people down to between one and four. I'll let your imagination handle that problem.

Pollution

What has happened is that not only have we in this country drifted into a profligately wasteful life-style with respect to everything we use, but because of the development of mass communications we're letting the whole world know that as far as we're concerned this is the appropriate way to live, and they're taking us at face value. But we haven't really thought through the significance of this.

What this means is that we are burning up energy at a terrific rate and producing pollution at a terrific rate, but the rest of the world—which, bear in mind, is nineteen times as many people as we are here in America—is being told by us that they should live the way we do. If they take us at face value, this means then that they very quickly want to move into a life-style that involves producing energy at the same rate per person we are, and producing pollution at the same rate we are.

Because we already have close to 55 cars per 100 people in the United States, our automobile population is only going up by 3.5 percent per annum. But in underdeveloped countries like Spain the automobile population is going up 8 percent per annum, which shows that the rate of buildup and production of pollution per person in this country is absolutely nothing compared to the rate of buildup of pollution per person in other countries.

This means that the clouds of pollution that you see very rapidly enlarging and coalescing in this country are building up at an even greater rate elsewhere.

Weather

This leads to another very interesting problem. Basically, human perception is very dull for processes which operate in such a way that some variable is fluctuating wildly about a gradually changing trend line. We become so impressed by the fluctuations that it's very difficult for us to notice that the trend line is gradually dropping or gradually rising; and, indeed, one of the most frightening things in the world at the moment is the fact that the weather is very obviously deteriorating internationally at the same time these clouds of smog are building up.

Now let me explain why I'm nervous about all this. A basic notion that mankind had through almost its entire history was that the world's weather was fundamentally determined by the position of the planets and the stars relative to each other. One of the first men who got the idea that this might not be correct was Benjamin Franklin. In 1783, just seven years before he died, Franklin made a very interesting observation. He noticed that that year, the sky in the United States (and he found also from his correspondence that this was true all over the world) was very, very cloudy and hazy, and in fact he couldn't get enough light with a magnifying glass to start a fire on a piece of paper.

And speculating about why this might be, and noticing that these hazy clouds were in fact not wet clouds, because no rain ever came out of them, but were rather dry hazy clouds, he got the very interesting idea that they might be fine ash from a volcanic eruption on an island off the coast of Iceland. In fact, he was only half right. In 1783 two of the three most gigantic volcanic eruptions of modern history went off: one was in Japan and the other was in Iceland. . . .

These eruptions put an immense amount of fine ash

into the upper atmosphere. It spread all over the world. The next time something like this happened was in 1816, when an eruption put so much fine ash into the upper atmosphere—in fact, thirty-eight cubic miles—that the entire world was chilled for about five years thereafter; 1816 was about the coldest year in the modern history books, and some of your parents or grandparents may have heard stories from their ancestors of the year people froze to death, or 1816, the year without a summer. This is a year that has imbedded itself deeply in the American consciousness. In fact, the whole world was affected to such an extent that by the summer of 1817, the highest asking price for a sack of flour on the London commodities market had risen to about 105 shillings, something more than double what its normal rate had been for several years previously. . . . International shipping was upset, world weather was upset enormously, and so on.

The next time scientists were attracted to the fact that there might be something odd about volcanic eruptions, of course, was when Krakatoa went off in 1883. This was the first time that the physics of the whole thing was doped out properly, and people were stimulated to do analyses of the whole history of the world's weather as long as we had weather records. One of the deans and pioneers of atmospheric physics, W. J. Humphries, found that these volcanic eruptions could put enough fine ash into the upper atmosphere to block out 20 percent of incoming solar radiation.

The key observation was that volcanic eruptions could have such a gigantic effect on the world's weather that they actually overrode the effect of the sunspot cycle. This research has planted in the minds of meteorologists and atmospheric physicists the realization that other events here on earth can have such a dramatic effect on the world's weather that they overcome any event of extraterrestrial origin. A number of people have begun to realize that man, through his manufacturing and transportation activities, is producing so much pollution that we are gradually moving to become the dominant influence on world's weather.

One of the first observations to suggest this was that in areas utterly remote from any local pollution source—such as the central Pacific Ocean, the Swiss Alps seventy-five miles from any city, the Caucasus in remote areas of Georgia in Russia, and over Kenya—the concentration of fine particles in the atmosphere has increased enormously in the last ten years. In the last couple of years, a few heavily instrumented aircraft have started flying all over the world to measure the concentration of fine particles in the atmosphere, and it's been discovered that these are building up very, very sharply. These are not just the particles that you can see from an airplane; these are particles that are sometimes so small that you cannot see them. And I would like to point out that all the discussion about control of air pollution by the new automobile emission devices is a lot of unutterable baloney. The most recently available devices have two effects: number one, if anything, they change the chemical mix of pollution emission; and, number two, they decrease the size of the particles by a factor of about ten. Both these things make the pollution more serious for health and for effects on weather than would be the case if we didn't try to alter it at all. So we're deluding ourselves. . . .

Coupled with this is an observation that's beginning to alarm meteorologists and geophysicists: the world has been chilling sharply for about twenty years. Some of you may be aware that last winter, at least in certain months, was one of the most brutal in the history of the last century. This was true in Tokyo, all over northern Russia, all over the northern part of western Europe, all over the British Isles, all over Canada; and it did such amusing things as far south as Florida as eliminating the walking catfish problem because walking catfish are tropical, and Florida had such a cold winter that they seem to have been largely annihilated.

The difficulty, of course, is that weather changes fluctuate a great deal from month to month and year to year, and the result is you can have a rather sharply changing trend line, and most people simply don't perceive this. For instance, New York City, where it ran twenty to thirty degrees Fahrenheit below the long-term mean for January, had a rather mild February, so few people realized that on balance since September 1, 1969, New York City has been running about two degrees below the long-term mean for the entire period.

If present trends continue, the world will be about four

degrees colder for the global mean temperature in 1990, but eleven degrees colder in the year 2000. This is about twice what it would take to put us into an ice age. The most reasonable explanation one can make of all the available evidence right up to the moment is that the cause is the constantly increasing mass of smog-produced clouds all over the world.

Noise

. . . It's very difficult to get information about something that is going to be very dangerous to us. . . . A few weeks ago the Sunday *Los Angeles Times* carried a full-page ad telling people about the wonders, from their short-term economic point of view, of buying homesites in an area called Palmdale, which is to be a proposed SST landing strip.

A little earlier on in the paper, there was an article explaining that the value of real estate had sunk to zero in an ever-increasing band of land around Los Angeles International Airport. The intensity and frequency of noises from all the jets landing and taking off meant that you couldn't live in the area, or conduct a business, or do anything else—you couldn't talk to anybody, you couldn't look at television, you couldn't listen to the radio, you couldn't do anything. And I think anybody who has been close to a major metropolitan airport will know that this is true.

Amusingly, of course, the SSTs are going to be vastly more noisy than the planes we have now, and therefore a supersonic airport is going to be vastly more noisy than the airports we have now. And this raises the question as to how or why the value of property right around a supersonic transport airport is going to go up when in fact the value of property right around the Los Angeles International Airport is down to zero. You literally can't sell it. You're bankrupt if you own property around the Los Angeles International Airport.

In fact, one expert group, the Environmental Quality Study Council of the state of California, which was appointed by the governor and the legislature, has come to the conclusion that there is an area in the center of the Los Angeles basin which is uninhabitable because of noise. It is gradually enlarging, so that within a few decades the entire Los Angeles basin will be uninhabitable; anybody who tries to inhabit it will be institutionalized.

Individual Decision Making

. . . Another fundamental problem with our society is what might be called the "American dream." That is an extension of the notion that persisted in the eighteenth and nineteenth centuries that it was more attractive to move west, that the solution of any problems you may have is always found somewhere else. The kind of thing this leads to is that while California, for example, grows 20 percent of the nation's citrus and Florida grows about 80 percent of the nation's citrus, California is essentially planning to go out of the citrus-growing business, because you can use the land much more profitably for "slurb" or tract housing. And Florida is planning to do the same thing. Florida assumes that California will grow the nation's citrus; California assumes that Florida will grow the nation's citrus.

The general principle here, of course, is that it's never in the economic interest of a part of a whole to do that which is in the interest of a whole. It is in our interest to grow citrus. Many epidemiologists argue that the development of the citrus-growing industry, coupled with the refrigerator car railroad system moving citrus all over the country, greatly reduced the infant mortality rate in this country in the twentieth century. It could be argued that we can synthesize vitamin C in our laboratories; it could also be argued that it may be difficult to make anything as pleasant a way of assimilating vitamin C as orange juice, and we diminish the quality of life thereby if we urbanize all of California and Florida. But neither one of them has a motive to operate on behalf of the whole country.

In fact, there is literally no investment as bad as an average acre of farmland for the purpose of farming. Agricultural economists have shown that that is just half as good as investing in an average share of common stock, and I don't think I need to give any of you a big song and dance to the effect that the average share of common stock is a pretty bad investment indeed.

However, on the other side, it is even more frightening

that there is scarcely anything you can do with money in this country that is as good as investing it in farmland for the purpose of converting it to urban use. In other words, anybody who is really investing in farmland for farming in this country is an economic martyr to the rest of the system. That is just insanity.

Now, so much for the difficulties in the decision-making process that each individual in our culture—I could obviously go on and on and on. But I have suggested enough things to indicate, I think, that it's difficult for the average human being in this country to make rational environmental decisions.

Institutional Decision Making

What I'd like to now do is to go on and consider a few examples of the additional difficulties that come about when human beings in our culture gather together, say, as members of the board of directors of a corporation, or members of a policy-making group such as a cabinet in a state or federal government.

All institutions have very real difficulties with the decision making, as three individuals in the last few years have been making clear to us in rather different ways. C. Northcute Parkinson has noted that all large institutions can take on goals that are utterly different from their stated goals.

John Kenneth Galbraith has said the same thing in a slightly different way. He's pointed out that organizations can become so compartmentalized that, in fact, the different compartments have no correspondence whatsoever to problems in the real world; and thereby the organizations become literally incapable of solving problems in the real world

Ralph Nader, in dealing with the ineptitude of institutions because of the way in which they are organized, has been doing something much deeper than what he appears to be doing. He is conducting experiments to test the hypothesis that large institutions are utterly incapable of solving the problems they are set up to solve. So, in effect, he's been going into competition with the decision-making arms, for example, of the large automobile manufacturers and parts of the government. And he's been in competition, for example, with the Food and Drug Administration. And guess who is more effective?

It is really difficult for all our large institutions to make intelligent decisions about anything, including environmental problems; and this suggests that it might be worthwhile for us to try to make a fairly penetrating analysis as to what these problems are. Let me give you an example of the kind of problem that one might think about with some interest.

You probably all know that luxury resort areas have a proclivity for going through cycles of overbuilding; and anybody, for example, who has been to Honolulu in the last couple of years has been struck by the fact that something very odd is going on. There probably has been no place in history where so many very large, expensive buildings were under construction at any given point in time, relative to the total number of buildings that were already there. And this has led people to wonder, some of them, where all the people were coming from to occupy these buildings.

This is similar to the situation with the airlines, which thought that they were going to build up their capacity enormously with the jumbo jets and the airbuses, and reduce their fares significantly because of the increase in volume. It's turned out, as you've noticed in the papers recently, that the airbuses and jumbo jets are actually going to be more expensive to ride around in than the conventional jets.

Just to show you how widespread this problem is, on one of the Hawaiian Islands in the last couple of years many of the hotels have been running occupancy rates as low as 2 percent per evening, which isn't extremely profitable. In July 1969, on this same island, a large development corporation announced that it was going to build 4,000 rooms of new hotel capacity and add 7,000 homes, which would just about have doubled the capacity of the island.

One might ask how we can possibly explain what seems to be absolutely blatant madness. . . .

Why are we building highways so rapidly when we obviously already have so much air pollution that highways are a tremendous problem for that reason alone? Why are we building more highways and freeways in our cities when it's obvious to any fool that the cities in which the traffic moves most rapidly are the ones that have rapid transit, and those in which it moves most slowly are the ones in which we have tried to solve our traffic problems by the highway-freeway system?

Why is it, for example, that people go to Los Angeles, see that about 44 percent of the total ground area of the city is committed to automobiles, yet at rush-hour traffic moves more slowly there than almost anywhere in the world? Why is it that we haven't perceived already that that is not the way to solve the problem?

Let me offer an explanation. If you think about the way decision-making groups are organized in large institutions, you'll notice that essentially decisions go through two layers of people. The first layer they go through is a policy-making body right at the top end of the organization: a cabinet or a board of directors. This policy-making body looks over an array of options that need to be considered, selects a subset of that whole array for consideration by its technical body, and then the subset is passed on to the technical body, which decides which of the remaining group of options is the one that the organization will proceed with.

The difficulty is that, if you analyze this phenomenon from a logical point of view, you see that one of the most important options ever confronted by a decision maker is what might be called the "no-go option," a decision not to proceed. And one of the things that almost invariably happens at one of these policy-making levels is that they either deliberately omit that option or forget that it exists. For instance, when did the Army Corps of Engineers decide that it wasn't going to build any dams this year? Or when did the state highway department decide it wasn't going to build any highways this year? When did the Senate Committee on Public Works decide it wasn't going to add to the interstate highway system this year? When did a financial or trust group that had money to spend on luxury resort hotels decide that it wasn't going to build anything this year?

It's this falling of the "no-go option" between stools, as it were, between the policy-making group and the technical group that makes decisions in a large organization, that leads to the fact that our society is so growth-oriented. Clearly we have to do something about this.

Another problem analogous to what Galbraith has pointed out, is that because our institutional decision-making bodies are compartmentalized around disciplines like economics, geology, zoology, and so on, they are typically incapable of seeing a problem whole. Now let me give you an example what this leads to.

It's well-known that about two-tenths of an acre of prime agricultural land is taken out of production all over the United States for each person added into the population. Now, most planning groups say that there is nothing to worry about in that, because even though we're reducing the acreage of prime agricultural land enormously every year, we'll enormously boost the production of the remainder by constantly increasing the inputs of agricultural technology. And another hidden implicit assumption (one of many made about this system) is that weather will remain constant. But I've already told you that it's highly unlikely that weather will remain constant; and it's also highly unlikely that we'll be able constantly to increase inputs of agricultural technology. So all our land-use planning is based on at least two hidden implicit assumptions which experts in the relevant fields consider to be wrong. I could rattle off a great list of hidden implicit assumptions about land-use planning like that.

The land-use planners have no input from meteorolgy or geophysics, but they also have no input from the people worrying about pollution or from the long-term energy planners in, say, the U.S. Geological Survey. What is happening, therefore, is that in all our large institutions we're making very, very important decisions about extremely complex issues on the basis of only a small part of the information that's really needed for such decision-making. And we simply have to stop that.

Another very serious problem in all our institutions is that decisions about what to do now are based on far too dim an understanding of what has happened in the past. Very quickly, I'd like to give you three examples of this, to illustrate how we can become so blinded by conventional wisdom that we have literally no idea what's going to happen in the future.

First, pesticides. The major charge that can be leveled against pesticides is not the pollution they cause. The major charge is that the notion they actually control pests is not fact. It's an assumption. It's part of the conventional wis-lom. Let me suggest that this assumption is wrong.

In the years after the Second World War, agricultural ntomologists in southeast Asia were driven frantic by the act that no matter what they did to control pests, the pests ept getting worse and worse and worse. And finally, in tter desperation, somebody got the idea a few years ago hat they might try to stop using pesticides. So he stopped sing pesticides and discovered to his utter amazement that e no longer had pests. Well, he thought, my God, this nust be some kind of an accident. He did experiments with he bagworm in oil-palm plantations. He applied pesti-ides to a particular point and measured subsequntly the oncentration of pests there and in all direction moving out om this point. He discovered to his utter amazement that e highest concentration of pests were where he had pplied the pesticide and that as he moved away from this lace the concentration of pests went down. This isn't quite e way it's supposed to work.

Another indication that there might be a fallacy in our inking about pesticides comes from the analysis of tree-unk rings in forested areas in New Brunswick. For as any centuries as you can go back there were pest out-eaks of the spruce budworm for about eight years at the d of every thirty-six-year cycle.

However, since 1945 we've sprayed many, many acres ith DDT every year. We've had a permanent outbreak nce 1945, an utterly novel situation. To give you an idea just how expensive that is, it costs between 60 cents and an acre to spray this stuff, and up to hundreds of ousands of acres and sometimes as many as two million res of this area have been sprayed every year. So we're ying a tremendous price—for what? We have a spruce dworm outbreak every year.

. . . Let me give you another example of how con-ntional wisdom can be wrong. When the white man left rope and went to other parts of the world, he always s confronted with two options, though he rarely recog-zed that he had these two options. One was to annihilate native plants and animals and bring over seeds and vestock from Europe and treat the new area as if it were other Europe. We had millions of buffalo in the Ameri-n West in the year 1800. These were slaughtered until there were only twenty-six animals left in 1888 and the American West was, in effect, converted from a grass–buffalo system to a grass–short–horn–Aberdeen Angus–Hereford system.

Well, the first time anybody twigged to the idea that maybe that was utter nonsense was a few years ago, when the owners of a big spread called the Henderson Ranch in southern Rhodesia decided that they wanted to do this same thing all over again. They paid some hunters to come in and shoot all the native game on this immense ranch so they could replace it with cattle imported from Europe. And to their utter horror, after paying the hunters to do this, the hunters were selling off the native game for more money per acre per year than the ranchers could have made by raising cattle on this same acreage. All of a sudden the light dawned. Maybe those plants and animals that have evolved at any given point on the Earth's surface over millennia have evolved there precisely because they are an assemblage of plants and animals which make utmost use of the energy from the sun and the minerals in the soil at that site. We've completely forgotten about Darwin and natural selection. . . .

In area after area after area we have done some very strange things. Computer simulation models show that cities exhibit what is called the "counterintuitive principle." That is, cities are so complex that if you deal with them in the way in which people deal with conventional problems—simple feedback problems such as sitting in the bathtub and turning the hot and cold faucets so the water is the right temperature—you typically do the wrong thing to a city. Having the very best of intentions, and doing the intuitively obvious thing to control a given problem, almost invariably gives you the wrong result. It exacerbates the problem you are trying to deal with.

In other words, society has become so complex that we need vastly more sophisticated means of dealing with its problems than we have been trying to use to this point.

There may be impediments to implementing planning even if the planning is good. Let's think about what a city really is. Suppose instead of having a city in the place where a city was you have a population of animals about the same size as human beings, and they lived on the plants and animals in an area surrounding the city. What would happen if that population grew so large that they exhausted the resources around the city?

Well, what Mother Nature always does in that case is to make the population subject to starvation. Starvation makes the birthrate go down; the death rate goes up, and consequently the population declines. What a scientist or an engineer would say about this situation is that the population was under tight feedback control. But what happens if a city gets too large for the resources surrounding the city?

Very simple. We make it uneconomical for the farmers to farm in the periphery surrounding the city, we have an explosion of suburbs all out into the farmland, and we take our food from increasingly greater distances. And everybody sits around and scratches his head and says, "Gee, that's funny, meat prices are going up." . . . And all of a sudden, food prices are skyrocketing in North America.

Some Solutions

Probably the most powerful single tool that a democracy has at its disposal for regulating itself is the tool of taxation. There are all kinds of gambits available to us by which we might manipulate tax legislation so as to produce literally any effect we want.

Our population is growing too fast; for a simple reason —everybody is encouraged to have lots of children. . . . In order to keep the U.S. population at its present level, the average American woman will have to confine herself to one child between now and the end of the century. . . . We simply have to use tax legislation, coupled with mass education, and of course abortion and everything else that is available to us, to induce families to reduce sharply the number of children they have. In fact, this is going to take an immense educational program and change the life-style of all people. In a cul-de-sac where five families live, we're going to have to encourage those five families to think of the five children the five famiiles have as being the children of all of them so that they have a complete family.

We're now encouraging people to take the short look. . . . We have to encourage them to take the "long" look. . . .

I'd like to make a plea—something that I've noticed and many, many other people who are traveling around the country a lot are noticing—certainly the younger congressmen are noticing it and some of the more astute senators are noticing it, and it was mentioned in the last issue of *U.S. News and World Report*—an extraordinarily dangerous thing is happening in this country at the moment.

More and more people are giving up on the system. This isn't just the young people, or the poor, or the black people. I've been startled to discover the extent to which white, middle-class, suburban housewives have become so frustrated and are so full of despair about the ability to have any effect on the system that they've given up on it. . . .

Democracy can't work this way. We're sowing the seeds of revolution if we assume that it is literally impossible for the average person in a democracy to have any effect on the system. We've got to become activist, but we've got to become activists in a positive way, and I suggest that there is a way to do this.

If there is an issue, or a number of issues, that are bothering you, this is what you can do about it. Read your newspapers carefully and see if a congressman or a senator or any other elected official is doing anything about this. Then face up to the fact that his time probably is very limited, his staff is very limited, and it would be extremely helpful to him to have volunteer help from the outside in structuring legislation or otherwise dealing with the problem. Then go to the library, do research on how best legislation can be structured to deal with this problem, make Xerox copies of any useful material that you find, and send these along to the senator or congressman or whoever it might be with a covering letter saying that you think this might be of help in structuring the legislation that will be most useful. Offer your services for further help of this sort, and explain exactly how your material can be of use. I think you will be absolutely thunderstruck at the response you get.

So, to conclude, I think America is now in a time of great crisis. We have two ways we can go. We can go the Santa Barbara way and start burning everything to the ground, or we can decide to become activists in a positive way and try to work within the system to correct these problems that we're dealing with, which have now very quickly moved us to the brink of disaster. I believe that Paul Ehrlich is not exaggerating when he says that we have about five more years at the outside to do something.

KENNETH WATT is an ecologist and professor of zoology at the University of California, Davis, Calif.

LAMONT COLE

IN UNISON

Kearney State College, Kearney, Nebr., April 22

. . . Man has been polluting the environment at least since Neolithic man began using fire as a tool, but a change in the whole magnitude of this process came about about three hundred years ago at the beginning of the Industrial Revolution, with the use of fossil fuels—coal, natural gas, and, more recently, petroleum. This put an entirely new dimension on changes in the environment, and we are continuing these changes at an accelerated rate. Now I know to many of you World War II seems a long time ago. It doesn't seem very long to me. Think just in this period since World War II of some of the entirely new classes of materials we've asked our environment to cope with—plastics, antibiotics, radionuclides, synthetic pesticides, and detergents.

A few years ago people were agonizing because suds were coming out of their faucets, so the chemists went back to the drawing board and came up with these so called biodegradable detergents that we use now. People couldn't see the detergents anymore, and they sat back and considered the problem solved. What they still don't realize is that these biodegradable detergents are more toxic to many forms of aquatic life than the old detergents were. They are phosphorus compounds. . . . And we use detergents at such a rate that, in the Northeast at least, phosphorous is our single most important water pollutant. The quality of phosphate in the U. S. rivers is reported to have increased by a factor of twenty-seven in very recent years.

Every now and then all of us become aware of a new form of pollution that we hadn't paid any attention to previously. Sweden has recently closed forty bodies of water to fishing, with the announcement that they can't consider even opening these for at least one hundred years. Then they'll take another look.

The problem in Sweden is mercury which has accumulated in the fish. The mercury had been used as a fungicide on seed, and it washed into the water. Japan has had several episodes of numerous human deaths from mercury poisoning and even more numerous deformed children born. In Japan the mercury came from plastics factories that released it into bays, and shellfish accumulated it.

Then we look around this country at the statistics on use of mercury, and we find that the U. S. is using more mercury, per capita and absolutely, than either Sweden or Japan ever have, so we may be on the verge of a very disheartening discovery.

Just last summer I became aware of a new class of compound, the polychlorinated biphenyls, or PCBs for short. These are very widely used in industry, in the plastics industry, in the rubber industry, and so on. The tons of rubber that wear off of tires in the U. S. every day are putting PCBs into the environment. Last summer I was serving on Secretary Finch's pesticide commission, and we were annoyed with PBCs because they interfere with the chemical test for chlorinated hydrocarbon pesticide residues.

But since then we've become aware that the PCBs are important pollutants in their own right. They undergo biological magnification just as DDT does, so that the predator accumulates a greater concentration of them than the prey that it was feeding on. And they have moved everywhere in the world. I talked last month to a man who was just back from Antartica, and PCBs have now turned up in the flesh of fish and penguins in Antarctica.

They are everywhere, and we can't even find the quantities produced, because these figures are shrouded in industrial secrecy. So it's hard to tell what we will discover next as a new environmental pollutant.

The U. S., with less than 6 percent of the world's population, is using something approaching 60 percent of the resources that are being consumed, and we're talking about industrializing the rest of the world after our own pattern. We are releasing into the environment more than 500,000 different chemicals and Paul Kotin, the director of the

National Institute of Environmental Health Sciences, is quoted last week as saying that this number of chemicals is increasing by more than five thousand per year.

I published a paper not too long ago in which I sought to answer the question, if we really try to keep our use of energy doubling every ten years—this is growth at the rate of 7 percent per year, which is the usual figure you hear in this country—how is the Earth going to get rid of all this heat? Because the heat has to ultimately be reradiated into space and to outer space, and in order to do this the Earth's surface will have to become warmer. And so I asked the question, How long will it take the Earth to become so hot it will be uninhabitable? If we go on increasing energy usage 7 percent per year.

Unfortunately I made a horrible error of arithmetic that made my figures come out much too optimistic. I thought that it was going to take about 800 years to make the Earth uninhabitable, but the correct figure is 130 years. And this is taking no account whatsoever of the greenhouse effect or anything like that that's taking place in the atmosphere. It's just the simple radiation balance of the Earth and outer space.

Not long ago Vincent Schafer, head of the laboratory of atmospheric sciences at the State University in Albany, published a paper summarizing some of his more than twenty-five years of monitoring the U. S. atmosphere. And I think the most striking thing that came out in his paper was the increase in air pollution upwind from our cities. I live fifty miles south of Syracuse, New York, a relatively small city of a quarter of a million people. I don't think that even ten years ago Syracuse could have been taken seriously as a regional source of air pollution; yet today we read in the paper that Cortland, New York, which is halfway between me and Syracuse, is threatening to sue Syracuse for polluting their atmosphere.

What is happening apparently is that the air that Syracuse receives from the west has already been to Buffalo and Rochester, and hasn't had time to become purified before Syracuse adds its contribution. So with our continuous growth, how long will it be before our East Coast megalopolis is adding to Europe's problem? Or if we seriously want to see the rest of Asia industrialized, how long will it be before pollution from Asia is adding to California's problem?

As a matter of fact, Reed Bryson of the University of Wisconsin has recently, with sophisticated instrumentation, been able to trace the flow of air pollution from Japan into California. You can't detect it visually yet but you already can with sophisticated instrumentation. And of course we know from the days of atmospheric testing of nuclear weapons that we can follow a cloud of pollution on several successive trips around the Earth. So if we really try to industrialize the rest of the Earth after our own pattern, we're going to be in very bad trouble here.

Frederick Smith, an ecologist at Harvard, has recently estimated the rate of environmental deterioration in this country at $30 billion per year. I think we can safely say that about a third of that should be allocated to water pollution. So $10 billion per year is an estimate of what it would cost us to stay even with pollution. This is not to clean anything up, but just to keep things from getting worse. Ten billion dollars a year.

The $2 billion a year that Mr. Nixon is proposing can't possibly do anything more than slightly reduce the rate at which things continue to get worse.

One trouble is that these environmental changes are so slow that people sort of become accustomed to them. I think if Lake Erie had changed overnight from the way it was fifty years ago to the way it is today, people would have realized that an ecological disaster had occurred and would demand that something be done about it. But they just became accustomed to seeing one beach after another closed to swimming, one fishing industry after another going out of business, and so on.

At the UNESCO conference in November, I received a paper that I think will give us a hint as to what sort of things we have to do to change our priorities here. Just as I was going on the program, a friend handed me a reprint from the *Journal of the American Medical Association* which I think is very informative. This paper was entitled something like "Hazard of Automobile Exhaust Gas on the City Streets." And in it the authors quoted the secretary of one of the largest automobile companies as follows:

"We are in business to build and sell automobiles. We'll worry about the public health aspects when the public demands it and legislation enforces it."

Now this is a little more forthright than we usually hear from public relations men, but I don't think it surprises any of you. All of you know the attitude. What I think may surprise you is the fact that this paper was published in 1923, forty-seven years ago we had our early warning about the automobile exhaust, and the companies are still dragging their heels. Since then they've made the engines larger and more powerful; they've increased the compression ratio, thereby adding nitrogen oxide to the inventory of pollutants. They've added lead to the gasoline, then boron, and more recently nickel, and heaven only knows what Madison Avenue will dream up next as a gasoline additive.

Our atmosphere itself is a biological product. Neglecting contaminants—99 percent of our atmosphere consists of just two gases—nitrogen and oxygen. And the only reason these gases are present in the atmosphere is that living things keep putting them there. Nitrogen is a scare element on Earth; there isn't very much of it except in the atmosphere. The reason it's there is that certain bacteria known as the denitrifying bacteria keep releasing nitrogen into the atmosphere, keep it cycling.

The only reason there is oxygen in the atmosphere is that green plants keep putting it there. They take in carbon dioxide and water and use the energy of sunlight through photosynthesis to release oxygen to the atmosphere. Now the most important of these plants in the oxygen cycle are the microscopic, free-floating green plants in the oceans which we call the marine phytoplankton. The reason for their great importance is this: a woods or a field of grass can produce tremendous quantities of oxygen, but when that wood burns or decays, or when the grass is digested by an animal, it uses up the same amount of oxygen that was produced in its formation.

The only way to compensate for the oxygen that we are using up in burning fossil fuels is to have green plants produce the oxygen and then have the remains of the plants sequestered away somewhere without being oxidized. Now this goes on in swamps and bogs and marshes, and to some extent in lakes—Lake Erie has one hundred feet of sediments with a very high oxygen demand in it down on the bottom. But the really big repository is in the oceans, in the marine sediments. And we are polluting our oceans.

If by any chance one of these half million chemicals, because the oceans of course are the ultimate sink for all 500,000 chemicals, should turn out to be a deadly poison for the marine phytoplankton, our atmosphere would start running out of oxygen. An alarming paper came out a little over a year ago by Charles Wurster at State University of New York in Stony Brook. He showed that DDT in low concentrations, a tenth of a part per million, could severely inhibit photosynthesis in the marine phytoplankton, at least those from Long Island Sound.

If this shoul turn out to be a general phenomenon, we may already be in trouble because if we stopped all use of DDT tomorrow, it would continue to wash into the oceans for several years, and most of it will go into coastal regions which are much more productive of life than the open ocean is.

You may recall last summer, when Thor Heyerdahl was trying to drift across the Atlantic, he expressed shock at finding the mid-Atlantic Ocean so visibly polluted with globules of unknown composition that the men were reluctant to dip their toothbrushes in the water. In the Pacific, something has set off a population explosion of a formerly rare starfish that gobbles up coral reefs. When the living corals are killed, the fish quickly disappear from the region and the beaches become subject to wave erosion, so some islands in the Pacific may literally disappear as a result of whatever man did to set off this population explosion.

Now we don't know what did it, but there's no doubt in my mind that man is responsible, probably through one of his pollutants or dredging activities. The reef at Guam is being destroyed at a rate of a half mile per month, and this starfish is also at work on Australia's Great Barrier Reef and in the Indian Ocean. Last summer for the first time we lost the entire catch of a marine fishery through pollution. I don't know why there was so much publicity for the seizing of the Coho salmon in Lake Michigan, because it's perhaps even more significant that we also seized the entire California catch of jack mackerel and declared it unfit for human consumption because of the presence of pesticide residues.

The navy has great plans for the ocean bottom. Sometimes they speak as though they want to turn it into an armed camp, and various countries are acting as though we're going to have a new colonial-type race for the resources of the ocean bottoms. The navy said about a year ago that American industry would be hesitant about investing in exploitation of the ocean bottom unless it could be assured of protection from piracy and foreign intervention.

This was a self-fulfilling prophecy because on September 30, 1969, a company that would like to mine manganese from the ocean bottom asked the navy for assurance that it would be protected from piracy and foreign intervention. And the navy seems only too happy to give such assurance. You may have read last summer that mustard gas, which the British disposed of in 1945 by dropping it into the Baltic, reappeared in 1969 injuring fishermen, threatening Baltic resorts, and causing the seizure and disposal of thousands of tons of fish.

You will recall that the U. S. Military has disposed of mustard gas itself, only in this case in the Atlantic Ocean, and more recently. The containers that our mustard gas is in are presumably still intact. And you may recall that only through the vigilance of a U. S. representative from New York State that the military was prevented from dumping nerve gas into the Atlantic Ocean.

It now begins to appear that the carrying capacity of this earth for human life will be determined not so much by its ability to produce food as by its ability to degrade waste. Our high standard of living that we're so proud of appears to be for this generation only. We are bequeathing you young people dying lakes, soil that is reduced in fertility, exhausted mineral deposits, and polluted oceans —plus such lovely things as these high-level nuclear wastes that are buried in Hanford, Washington, and down in the Savannah River, South Carolina and in Idaho.

These wastes are so hot that one estimate has been that they will boil spontaneously for three-hundred years. The Atomic Energy Commission has these in tanks of stainless steel and concrete where they are constantly cooled. AEC's own survey a couple of years ago showed about 5 percent of these tanks to be leaking after only about twenty years. There's a big item in the AEC budget this year for new tanks to replace those that are leaking. Now AEC says themselves that this material must be kept from polluting the environment for at least six hundred years, so here's what we are leaving you: millions of gallons of this stuff with instructions to keep it out of the environment for six-hundred years, and to change the tanks it is stored in at your expense every twenty years.

And then think about how many governments have even survived for six-hundred years. Our decision here is that we make all of our decisions on the basis of short-term economic considerations. Today we are seeing the no-deposit, no-return bottle. In fact, in the town where I live all the grocery stores have put up signs, that they won't accept any deposit bottles. Statistics show that a deposit bottle makes an average of twenty round trips, so by this one move, we are increasing this particular solid-waste disposal problem by a factor of twenty.

We have legislation that gives depletion allowances, which encourages mining with all of its detrimental environmental effects. If our legislators would make it as expensive to mine and refine new ore as it is to reclaim used metal, those automobile graveyards would disappear and discarded beer cans would be much less in evidence. Even farming is industrialized. My grandfather was an Illinois farmer; he never bought synthetic fertilizers. In fact, he practiced crop rotation and his animals were out on the field spreading manure, and what they didn't spread, he did. And this went along very nicely.

But now on that same land, everything is changed. Economically the thing to do now is crowd your animals into feed yards, perhaps hundreds of cattle per acre. Feed them there; use synthetic fertilizer on your fields, and then worry about the waste disposal problem with the animal waste. Actually two billion tons of this animal waste produced every year is second in volume only to sediment as a solid waste disposal problem.

Let me give you one more example, the decision to build the supersonic transport, the SST. This plane is expected to fly around at an altitude of 65,000 feet. This is well up in the stratosphere. There's no weather up there. No turbulence. No precipitation. Nothing to wash air pollutants out. We know from some volcanic eruptions in historic times that particulate matter in the stratosphere takes on the average perhaps two years to settle out. So now what happens when you get a thousand SSTs flying around up there? This is not an exaggeration. I saw one projection by Boeing of 1,200 SSTs to be sold, the French and British are estimating 600, and so on. Vincent Schafer, a meteorologist from Albany, has made some calculations on this, and he's talking about the global gloom that may settle over the entire Earth as a result of the SST.

You heard about the sonic boom but this is a minor problem compared with stratospheric pollution. Now let me recall for you why the decision was made to go ahead with the SST. You certainly can't justify it on speed of travel. What good does it do you to save two hours on a transatlantic flight when your boss is going to tell you not to conduct any business for twenty-four hours anyway, because you've put your biological clock out of phase. This won't justify the SST.

The decision was made solely on the basis of dollar exchange. We must not let the British and French and Russians corner the market for these things, so that our airlines would have to buy from them; instead we must produce the plane so their airlines will have to buy from us.

The basic problem underlying all of these things, of course, is the problem of the population explosion. Mankind is like cancer cells that don't know when to stop multiplying.

I published my first despairing paper on the population explosion twenty-one years ago and I'm getting a little tired of the subject. The way we're going now, the population will double again every thirty-five years and there's just no possibility that the Earth environment can stand the pressures that we'll be putting on it.

Now I've also heard it said that the U.S. does not have a population problem, because our population is only growing at 1 percent per year, as compared to 2 percent in India and 3 percent in some Latin American countries, and so forth. I say however that our population explosion in this country may be the most serious one in the world because in terms of the resources that he will use up in his lifetime, the pollution he will cause, and so on, one American is the equivalent of about eighty Indians.

In all these years of talking about the population explosion, I still occasionally come up with a new perspective that makes me realize again the vertical rise of the curve of world population. I wonder if it will startle you to have somebody tell you that there are living right now on Earth approximately 4 percent of all the people who have ever lived on Earth, from the first cavemen, through the Egyptian empires, through the Roman Empire, through the Middle Ages, right up till now. This is our most serious problem and yet Stewart Udall, former secretary of the interior, recently testified before a congressional committee that the amount of money the U.S. spends annually on population regulation at home and abroad would run the Pentagon for three hours. I mentioned this to a man who is very knowledgeable in government circles, and he said, "I'm sure those three hours must refer to a Sunday afternoon."

In his state of the union message, President Nixon asserted that 100 million children will be born in the U.S. between now and the turn of the century. I hope that this was not a self-fulfilling prophecy because it presupposes continuing population growth at just about our present rate. I'd feel much happier if President Nixon had said we will make it a matter of policy to see that no more than 50 million children are born in the U.S. before the turn of the century.

Now I'm no sociologist or psychologist, but I can't be convinced that many of our other problems are unrelated to this crowding and continuous growth. The violence in our cities, the rise of mysticism with everybody wanting their own guru, the multiplication and expansion of the astrology columns in our papers. Yes, and the attempts to get away from it all through the use of drugs. People sense that something is wrong, they are desperate and don't know what to do about it.

Now I've been attending enough of these environmental teach-ins to get a feeling for some of the directions that the discussion may go, and ever since I became aware of these directions, I've been trying to advise these young people. Because one direction it often goes is toward blaming all our problems on private enterprise and the profit motive. And I tell these students I hope they will not settle for any such simplistic explanation.

In the first place, I know a good deal about environmental degradation in Russia and their problems are identical with ours. It's not the type of government, it's the passion for continuous growth, keep everything expanding, which has been called the Chamber of Commerce syndrome. In the second place, one of the very largest sources of environmental deterioration in this country is our own government. Now I could spend a good many hours telling you what I think you ought to know about the army corps of engineers, the Bureau of Reclamation, some parts of the Department of Agriculture, not to mention the Department of Defense—where 40 percent of our total federal expenditure is going into the methods and techniques of destruction.

But I want today to speak about just one agency because I have some new information here, and I want to take this chance when I have an international audience to say a little bit about the Atomic Energy Commission.

Now among the other radionuclides that are released to the environment is tritium, radioactive hydrogen. The AEC takes tritium so lightly that it doesn't even monitor the amount being released into the environment from many of their own installations. Some of the national laboratories don't even monitor it. Tritium has a very feeble beta ray emission that will only travel a fraction of a millimeter in water. This makes it hard to monitor and is the reason AEC has taken it so lightly.

But the trouble with tritium is that it is hydrogen and it gets built into water, and it goes everywhere that ordinary water goes, including into and through the bodies of all living things, plants and animals. It gets built into their organic compounds, including the nucleic acids that carry the genetic information for the next generation. This may be a feeble little beta ray, but if it's being emitted right inside of your genes, the results can be disastrous.

For all practical purposes, tritium did not exist on Earth thirty years ago, so here's something that we know can cause genetic damage, and that we have no long-term experience with. Yet we are risking the release of enormous quantities of this to the environment. One new nuclear plant that's going in at Calvert Cliffs, Maryland, is going to release at least seven thousand curies of tritium per year into Chesapeake Bay.

On November 20, 1969, I testified before the U. S. enate subcommittee on air and water pollution, which as holding hearings on the use of nuclear explosives for xcavation. In that testimony I showed the figures pubshed by the Atomic Energy Commission itself, that made possible to calculate that just to dig one canal, the proosed sea-level canal across Panama, would release to the eneral environment of the Earth, initially to the atmoshere among other things over a billion curies of tritium nd a quarter million curies of strontium 90.

I pointed out that the International Commission on adiological Protection sets guidelines giving a maximum ermissible burden for the whole human body for persons ccupationally exposed to each radionuclide, and I pointed ut that the amount of tritium released in digging this one anal would provide the maximum permissible whole body urden for about a trillion persons, approximately three undred times the present world population of the Earth. he quarter million curies of strontium 90 would be the aximum body burden for 125 billion persons, or about irty times the present human population.

I mentioned these two nuclides, which are actually a ery small fraction of what would be released, merely beause they prove that nuclear explosives can't be made ny cleaner. If you increase the proportion of fusion in the evices, you increase the amount of tritium produced. If ou reduce the proportion of fusion in the device, you inease the amount of strontium 90 produced. But the AEC back in an era of thought that might have been acceptable ecologists two generations ago when it was a truism to y that the solution to pollution is dilution.

Their standard for radioactivity is simply how dilute ou can make it, not how much of it you pour out. I bring is up now because the current issue of the trade journal, *iomedical News,* dated April 1970, quotes a coordinator a study for AEC as saying the Panama Canal project ooks to us as though it could be done without exceeding urrent radiation standards." But two days before I testified efore that subcommittee, they took testimony from Dr. ohn Gofman, associate director of the Lawrence Radiation aboratory in California, who is both a nuclear physicist d a physician, and his colleague Dr. Arthur Tamplin, calling for an immediate reduction in the permissible radiation levels by a factor of at least ten.

Just a few days after I testified, I received a transcrip for editing and I promptly returned it. Normally the tran scripts of these hearings would have been published lon ago, but these have not been. A magazine editor who calle to ask for transcripts told me that she was told that AEC was taking time to prepare rebuttals, which in my experience is a totally new procedure. The same issue of *Biomedical News* that I've referred to reports that politica pressure has resolved the issue in favor of nuclear advocates. They're going ahead to dig this Panama Canal wit nuclear explosives.

I'm happy to be speaking to an international forum. Th protests of the U.S. senators and representatives, not t mention scientists, have been unable to retard the irresponsible determination of one U.S. government agency to release into the general world environment toxins in quantities representing several lethal doses for every person o Earth. Our problems are global, not national. We are obviously unable on a national level to restrain powers tha are working to make the Earth uninhabitable.

I hope that before it is too late, if it isn't already, a peoples will insist in unison upon the theme that man schools have adopted for this Earth Day: Give Earth chance.

LAMONT COLE is a professor of ecology and biological scienc at Cornell University.

GARRETT HARDIN

TRAGEDY OF THE COMMONS

University of Illinois, Circle Campus, Chicago, Ill.
April 22

We have to watch out for people who have vested interests or who are merely caught in the rut of ancient ways of thinking, disguising the truth by a misuse of language. Much of this disguise we see is merely the result of ancient ways of thinking that haven't been reexamined. And it's this latter aspect of the problem that I particularly want to talk to you about today. In doing this I want to make use of a "scenario" that was written more than a hundred years ago by an Englishman named William Lloyd. This scenario I will call the "tragedy of the commons."

Imagine, Lloyd says, a common field open to all herdsmen who have cattle. Each herdsman keeps his own bunch of cattle, has them branded, and at the end of the season he gathers in his cattle to sell and take the profits. The pastureland is a commons open to all. Now as you probably know, each particular pastureland has a maximum "carrying capacity," and if you exceed that maximum capacity, you get not more proceeds, but less. So let us imagine that this commons is already being run at its maximum carrying capacity.

At this point one of the herdsmen thinks he might add one more animal to his herd, and he debates, should he or should he not? Acting as a completely rational person he asks, What have I to gain? What have I to lose?

What he has to gain is the eventual sale of one more cow at the end of the season. So that's pretty good. What he has to lose is the loss from overpasturing the commons. But this loss is shared among all the herdsmen. He doesn't pay for this by himself; they all pay for it. And so the loss to him is very slight. Consequently, he says, the only rational thing for me to do is to add one more cow to my herd, because I gain one more cow when I sell it and I lose only a little bit in the meantime because of overpasturing.

But this same sort of reasoning implies also that he should add two more, and three more, and four more, and so on, without limit. The same type of reasoning is used by every other herdsman. The result is that they all add more to their herd, and destroy the commons through overgrazing.

Now the important thing to notice about this is that each man is behaving rationally; each man makes a rational decision when he adds to his herd, a rationally correct decision. And yet the final consequences of all these individually correct decisions is complete destruction of the commons. Since they are all locked into this system, since they cannot avoid this, I speak of their situation as a *tragedy* of the commons. A tragedy is any course of events which individuals are powerless to prevent, so long as they play the game by the rules.

This insight of Lloyd's explains why it is that private property is superior to commons in a crowded world. Under a system of private property where each herdsman owns the pastureland on which his cows graze, the individual is responsible for what happens. He has an *intrinsic* responsibility, because if he makes the wrong decision he's going to suffer from it. He's going to destroy his own pastureland, whereas when the pastureland is shared by all, he does not have that intrinsic responsibility and essentially his responsibility is zero. As a matter of fact, you might say it's worse than that in the commons because he actually has to gain by mistreating the commons.

This type of analysis is needed to call our attention to the fact that in terms of their pure forms there are really three basic political systems and not two, as we're usually led to believe. We're usually led to believe that the only choices are private enterprise and communism. But you see, the commons is a system utterly different from either one of these, and is really worse than either.

We need to label this type of a system with a name so that we can speak of it, so that we can discuss it intelligently. And until we do get this label, people are going to continue to suffer from verbal pollution, continue to be misled by improperly used words.

For example, I am sure all of you have seen at some time or other an advertisement showing a fancy, electronically equipped ship plowing through the ocean with all sorts of gear for catching fish. This ad includes a statement of this sort: "Feeding the poor of the world from the inexhaustible wealth of the seas through the benefit of American private enterprise."

Now that is a bunch of crap. In the first place, we don't feed the poor of the world. Only 17 percent of the fish from the oceans go to the poor countries of the world (and even there they probably go to the wealthy people). Yet the poor countries constitute 67 percent of the world. That's the first falsehood in the statement. The second falsehood is that the wealth of the seas is "inexhaustible." This is not true. We have heard before of the inexhaustible wealth of the American forests, of the inexhaustible game on the American prairies. Every one of the inexhaustibilities has been or is being exhausted.

The same thing is true for the oceans of the world. Though at present cropped only to about a third of the extent they could be, the oceans also have limits. The wealth of the oceans is *not* inexhaustible.

The third falsehood is that the harvest is being reaped through the glories of American private enterprise. The exploitation of the oceans is not a matter of private enterprise; neither is it communism. Oceans are being treated as a commons. All of us—Americans, Russians, Japanese, Peruvians—everybody who's out there in the ocean getting fish out of it is exhausting the commons, and we are all locked into a system that has no end except tragedy. There is nothing we can do, each one of us acting rationally, except exhaust the wealth of the oceans. Then we will all be worse off than we are now.

The only thing we can possibly do is to change the rules, and no doubt some day we will. At the present time we don't see how to, principally because we have no international organization to make rules that we will accept. So in the meantime, all of us are playing out this game of the tragedy of the commons in the oceans of the world.

GARRETT HARDIN is a professor of biology and biological science at the University of California, Berkeley, Calif.

WALTER F. MONDALE

COMMITMENT TO SURVIVAL

University of Minnesota, April 22

Every five to twenty years, an extraordinary phenomenon takes place in Scandinavia. The lemmings, for reasons unknown, begin their suicidal march to the sea.

We are not unlike this little creature—seemingly bent on the destruction of his own species.

The only real differences are that we don't wait ten years between marches, and we seem determined to take every other creature along with us.

I wonder what would happen if we sent out a questionnaire—which, incidentally, is one of the things we do best in this country—to all the other animals in the kingdom asking whether or not they would be upset if their brother, *Homo sapiens,* were to disappear from the Earth. My guess is that we would get back a nearly unanimous answer that not one among them would shed a tear for our passing, since we have created such an unlivable environment for them. Except, maybe, the dog who is sort of the Uncle Tom of the animal kingdom.

Earth Day is *our* day as a nation—because it is we who are being awakened to the profound crisis of our environment. We are awakening to:

* Lakes and rivers, fouled by sewage, poisoned by industrial wastes, and suffocating in algae;
* Air turned black by 142 million tons a year of smoke and fumes;
* A countryside violated with concrete, asphalt, and neon; and strewn with the yearly remnants of 48 billion cans, 28 billion bottles, 30 million tons of waste paper, and 7 million junked cars;

* Twenty-two species of wildlife gone forever and another eighty waiting the end of their species . . . "Not with a bang but a whimper";
* The oceans, so seriously polluted that scientists predict the end of their productivity in ten to twenty years;
* And a generation of young people who carry "strontium 90 in their bones, asbestos in their lungs, idoine 131 in their thyroid, and DDT in their fat."

There are some who hope your concern for the environment, shown here today, means that you will forget about the other symptoms of our discontent.

"The environment," to them, is a "healthy" diversion—a new trick—to occupy restless minds and bodies during spring. "Let the amateurs clean up America and leave the professionals alone to clean up southeast Asia."

But they are wrong.

The crisis of environmental decay is clearly bound to the crises of poverty, blight, racism, war, and economic injustices.

Our "environment" includes:

* The mangrove fields of South Vietnam, made barren for a generation by 50,000 tons of herbicides;
* "The environment" is a deprived child, stunted in mind and body from disease, hunger, and a world without hope;
* "The environment" is people—well over 200 million now, with 5,500 born each day, jamming into the cities, neglecting the towns and rural areas;
* "The environment," in the words of the Kerner Commission, is "two societies, one black, one white—separate and unequal";
* "The environment" is violence . . . as the Eisenhower Commission told us: "making fortresses of portions of our cities and dividing our people into armed camps";
* "The environment" is a mood of retreat—encouraged by some in high office—which would replace urgency and idealism with self-interest and "benign neglect";
* "The environment" is a federal budget which allocates:
  —$106 million for air pollution and $3.4 billion for space programs;

—$200 million to feed hungry children and $290 million for the SST;
—$800 million for the preservation of our water and $1.5 billion for the second stage of ABM;

* Most of all, "the environment" is a culture which seems to value:
—quantity above quality;
—self-interest, convenience, and expediency above the beauty and mystery of nature;
—and the preservation of institutions above all well-being and full opportunity of men they were born to serve.

Twelve years ago, John Kenneth Galbraith described this culture in his brilliant book *The Affluent Society*. He wrote:

> The family which takes its mauve and cerise, air conditioned, power-steered, and power-braked automobile out for a tour passes through cities that are badly paved, made hideous by litter, blighted buildings, billboards, and posts for wires that should long since have been put underground. They pass on into a countryside that has been rendered largely invisible by commercial art. They picnic on exquisitely packaged food from a portable icebox by a polluted stream and go on to spend the night at a park which is a menace to public health and morals. Just before dozing off on an air mattress, beneath a nylon tent, amid the stench of decaying refuse, they may reflect vaguely on the curious unevenness of their blessing. Is this, indeed, the American genius?

This, then, is the nature of the task before us. It is more than raking up our own backyards, more than getting the phosphates out of detergents, developing biodegradable containers, or cracking down on industrial polluters.

The task calls for some fundamental changes in these economic habits, social values, and national priorities.

Consider, for example, the magnitude of the crisis in water.

Probably no single resource is as precious to the people of Minnesota as their lakes and waterways.

Yet, every day we pour 25 billion pounds of human,

chemical, and industrial wastes into our nation's lakes and rivers. Two million pounds of pesticides, and over 104 million pounds of fertilizer are added to the land each day, to find their way into the nearest waterway and feed the growth of green algae.

Lake Erie is already dead, killed by the steady discharge of poison at the rate of one ton per minute.

The Mississippi, south of St. Louis, is so toxic that signs warn against eating food *near* the banks.

Ohio's Cuyahoga River flowed so thick with oil scum that it caught fire.

According to Gaylord Nelson: "We have in the last forty years polluted every major watershed in America east of the Mississippi to a serious degree, and every major watershed west of the Mississippi to some degree."

Here in Minnesota:

* The magnificent Lake Superior, the third greatest body of fresh water in the world, is threatened with 60,000 tons a day of taconite tailings—only a single example of our abuse of that lake;
* The Boundary Waters Canoe area—with some of the purest water and most unspoiled land in the nation—is threatened by mining interest which would cash in this irreplaceable wilderness for a possible profit in metal;
* The Mississippi, where it is not yet spoiled by chemical and organic discharge, is threatened at Monticello by thermal heat and radioactive discharge;
* Hundreds of our 14,000 lakes are threatened by eutrophication. We have already seen our precious freshwater community lakes fill up with slime and algae which feed upon the nitrates and phosphates washed in from fertilizers, detergents, and sewage. . . .

First of all, we must as a nation stand ready *now* to commit the vast resources needed to undo a history of abuse and neglect—not the vague token commitment of $4 billion spread over the next ten years as promised by the administration.

The *New York Times* estimated the cost of cleaning all the nation's waterways at $100 billion. Out of sight? We have already spent that much in Vietnam.

Gaylord Nelson of Wisconsin has called for a commitment of $20-$25 billion a year. Impossible? Studies by the Brookings Institution and by the Joint Economic Committee suggest that our defense budget could be cut by $10-$20 billion with no real loss in defense capability. In fact, if we had simply been able to prevent the monstrous cost overruns on thirty-eight weapons systems now in progress, we would have saved $21 billion. That much alone would have met the five-year goal set in 1968 by the Federal Water Pollution Control Agency. And that sum would represent less than the $24 billion we spent getting a man to the moon . . . which we found so far to be much cleaner but far less hospitable than the Earth.

It's time to apply a little "law and order" to the industries, municipalities, and individuals who are fouling our environment.

The laws are on the books. But the regulations are inadequate, the penalties often insufficient, and the enforcement tragically lacking.

Radioactive pollution, for example, is a growing threat with 80 million gallons of radioactive wastes already buried in our country—there to remain for an active life of up to twenty thousand years.

But disposal and regulation is carried out by the AEC—which is also the chief *promoter* of atomic power. Their priorities may be revealed in the one-fifth of 1 percent of their budget spent on disposal research, and the one-half of 1 percent spent on regulation. They have jealously resisted Minnesota's efforts to set her own stricter standards for radioactive safety.

Another example of inadequate regulation and enforcement is automobile pollution.

The auto is the greatest air polluter of them all, causing about 60 percent of all air pollution, and adding some 90 million tons of pollutants a years to our atmosphere, filling the air with lead, carbon monoxide, hydrocarbons, and two hundred other chemicals.

But for the past seventeen years, according to Department of Justice officials, the major auto companies had engaged in a conspiracy to prevent the development and installation of effective pollution control devices.

Evidently, the auto makers have promised to be good in the future, because the charges were dropped and settled out of court. Now we are relying on law that sets emission standards only on the newest cars, and monitors only the prototypes sent by the manufacturers for testing.

Eight years ago, Rachel Carson wrote *Silent Spring*, and the world awakened to the terrifying danger of DDT—a persistent poison accumulating in the fat of virtually all creatures on earth.

We know that DDT causes abnormalities of eggshells, birth defects in fish, cancer in mice, and disastrous damage to insect ecology.

Denmark, Sweden, Finland, Great Britain, Hungary, Germany, and the Soviet Union have already banned the use of DDT and other chlorinated hydrocarbons. The United States has allegedly banned the use of DDT, but it is allowing the continued production, marketing, and release of over 25 million pounds of this poison while challenges and appeals are going on.

Even more shocking for their direct effect on human beings are the organophosphates. These poisons take an estimated annual toll of 800 deaths and 80,000 injuries to farm workers brought into contact with them.

While farm workers are struck down by chemicals structurally similar to nerve gases used in chemical warfare, the state and federal departments of agriculture argue about "legal tolerance limits." . . .

* * *

In his final speech to the United Nations, Adlai Stevenson said:

> We travel together, passengers on a little spaceship, dependent on its vulnerable reserves of air and soil; all committed for our safety to its security and peace; preserved from annihilation only by the care, the work, and the love we give our fragile craft.

SENATOR MONDALE is a Democrat from Minnesota.

PART II

PROMISES, PROMISES

Frankly, the two hundred American boys who died in Vietnam last week don't care anymore whether the air is dirty or clean.

—Representative George Brown
University of California at Los Angeles
April 22

ADLAI E. STEVENSON III

Too Little, Too Late

Western Illinois University, Macomb, Ill., April 22

Thirteen years ago I visited Albert Schweitzer in Africa and asked him what disturbed him most about the world. He replied without hesitation that man had for the first time acquired control over the very elements but still had not acquired control over himself. So that old man had gone off to what was then French Equatorial Africa where he ran a primitive hospital and played Bach on the organ at night in the stillness of the jungle. He is dead now and spared the spectacle of what we have since done to ourselves through the accumulation of weapons and the by-products of rampant technology.

But perhaps there is more hope now. We sense that our continued failure to control ourselves has placed man, himself, on the endangered species list. We fear that if we do not go out with a bang or a whimper, it may be with a cough. We have reached for the moon and beyond, and looking back through space we have been confronted by the insignificance of the planet which sustains us. . . .

We have not had the time, nor the knowledge in some cases, nor the inclination to perceive what our growth has done to us, let alone deal with the problems our growth has created. The Gross National Product was our holy grail. We have prized production, speed, inventions, bigness, newness. We have celebrated numbers showing increases in the population, automobiles, size of our cities. We've been concerned with quantities of goods and services and not with the quality of life, not with tranquillity, cleanliness, privacy, and human understanding of one another. . . .

It is the purpose of the political process to make those

choices, to require that the costs are paid and to help pay the price—to translate the people's needs into public policies. The technical papers, the research studies, the program proposals, and the concerns of an aroused people must become the policies of our land. . . .

Since politics is the cutting edge, let's look at the choices being made by the administration in Washington. All that we discuss here amounts to nothing unless the national budget is altered, our priorities reordered, unless federal legislation is enacted, unless local, state, and national governments act.

* In fiscal 1969 we spent more on the flight of Apollo 11 than on federal air and water pollution programs combined;
* The federal government spends more on the war in Vietnman two weeks than it has spent on air pollution control in the past ten years;
* Mr. Nixon requested over twice as much to promote the SST next year as to control air pollution.

We must do more than talk about the environment. . . . Let me give you a few examples of talk and no action, for this administration has asked to be judged by its deeds, not its words:

Clean-water grants to help towns and cities build needed waste treatment plants were authorized by Congress back in 1966 to be $1.2 billion this coming year. The federal government, itself, has said it will take at least $4 billion just to clean up Lake Michigan. Our Illinois stream cleanup will be at least another $5 billion. Yet the Nixon administration proposes $800 million for water treatment.

Automotive air pollution accounts for 60 percent of the nation's air pollution and for as much as 90 percent in some cities. Although the president admits this form of air pollution is particularly insidious, he calls for a cut in the research budget for the automotive problem—a cut from $45 million appropriated this year to only $28 million. Nor is the air pollution agency going to be allowed to spend the full amount appropriated this year.

Enforcement of federal air and water pollution control laws today is arbitrary, cumbersome, and inadequate. Enforcement takes money, too—money to collect information on water and air quality and money to determine who and what affects water and air quality. . . . Since Mr. Nixon has been in Washington, only twelve actions have been filed to enforce the Federal Water Pollution Control Act and the Clean Air Act. And we will not see significant increase with the funds requested.

If we had more than fourteen federal inspectors patrolling offshore oil-drilling operations, the oil pollution tragedies to the Gulf of Mexico and to the Louisiana coast might have been averted. And do you think there will be a real investigation of offshore oil drilling when many of Mr. Nixon's investigators are appointed from the investigated? It seems unlikely to me that the Union Oil Company will take a very hard look at the Union Oil Company.

Enforcement must cease being a political log rolling operation. It should be systematic and automatic, based on our need for clean water and air and on violations of laws and standards. Those who violate these standards should know that a federal action will follow.

Urban parks are badly needed in our cities and in our surrounding suburban areas, where most Americans now live. President Nixon—under pressure from Congress—has reversed his "no-new-parks" policy that he followed last year. But he would budget for the urban parks program a meaningless amount—$75 million for cities where land is expensive.

. . . Today, the national pollution control programs are negative in approach. Before the government can act to control damage, that damage to the air or water must have occurred. The programs even sound negative—it's a "pollution control" program not a clean-water and clean-air program. This too little, too late approach is tantamount to writing an obituary instead of preventing a murder.

The federal government, itself, is on this treadmill of destruction. Federal agencies sponsor activities through loans, grants, contracts, leases, and licenses which pollute the water, foul the air, gouge the landscape, and destroy its beauty and wildlife. While the administration talks about the environment, it is issuing offshore oil-drilling leases, issuing permits and giving contracts to industries, constructing airports and highways, dredging harbors, building dams—with no adequate requirement that these activities be conducted in a way that protects the environment.

The federal government cannot in good conscience require pollution controls of others if it is not practicing good environmental management in its own policies and programs. The current administration has completely neglected this conflict between its policies to control pollution and its programs which contribute to pollution. Environmental protection should always be included particularly in federal programs for transportation, agriculture, national defense, industrial and city development. A preventative strategy could begin by requiring the federal government and those who do business with it to observe the highest standards to preserve our environment. . . .

The federal government should give grants to cities, towns, or regional organizations to help them improve disposal operations and enable them to install equipment to sort out usable elements for reuse. Research and development should be tripled over the present meaningless levels. We must find cheaper and better approaches to solve this enormous problem.

In addition to all its other inadequacies the federal government's approach to environmental quality is fragmented. One department has the air pollution control program, another has the water pollution program, still another has the urban parks program. In addition to the agencies administering the major programs, other agencies have minor parts of air or water pollution control, open spaces and recreation and wildlife and soil management. Altogether, seventeen different departments and agencies operate environmental quality programs. This approach guarantees fragmented understanding of the environment. No priorities are set for spending in these programs, based on national problems and needs. . . .

The cost overrun on one torpedo—the Mach 48—will exceed all federal spending in fiscal 1970 for elementary education, secondary education, and water pollution combined. This madness must come to an end. It is inconceivable that one such weapon system is more vital to our security and well-being than the preservation of our water resources. And I might as easily have mentioned the C5As, the F-111s, the unworkable missile systems, the superfluous aircraft carriers, or the main battle tank. In the decade just ended we spent $650 billion in the name of national security and indeed are less secure than when we began. Let us remember in the decade ahead that our true security depends upon energies of human redemption and salvation as well as upon those of death and destruction.

Governments act in response to pressure. Too often the pressure comes from everyone except the people. The politicians are represented, the polluters are represented, but what of the people? That is up to you—and why we are here today. The fight against pollution cannot be separated from the need for leadership and the need to make our political institutions more responsive to the people. New ideas must be heard—new pressures must be felt. . . .

ADLAI STEVENSON is the treasurer of the state of Illinois.

GAYLORD NELSON

War Games

University of Wisconsin, Madison, Wis., April 21

Our goal is an environment of decency, quality, and mutual respect for all other human creatures and for all other living creatures. An environment without ugliness, without ghettos, without discrimination, without hunger, without poverty, and without war. . . .

This will require some tough decisions—political, economic, and social decisions that I am not certain the majority of people in this country support.

In terms of dollars it will not cost a mere two or three billion, but a commitment of $25—30 billion a year, and soon thereafter a commitment of $40—50 billion dollars a year.

Twenty-five to thirty billion dollars sounds like a lot of money. It is. It is equal to the amount we are wasting on a mistaken enterprise in Vietnam right now.

Twenty-five to thirty billion dollars is less money than we will end up spending on a equally mistaken enterprise—the antiballistic missile. . . .

We are a creative society with a great capacity for inventing reasons why we can't live with the Russians. And the Russians are equally creative in inventing reasons why they can't live with us. I suggest that neither of us will survive in any acceptable condition unless we are all prepared to put our petty war games aside and start dealing with matters that are important to the human enterprise.

Senator Nelson is a Democrat from Wisconsin.

WILLIAM B. SPONG, JR.

Dollars and Sense

Mary Baldwin College, Staunton, Va., April 22

. . . Anger has been helpful. It has already aroused the country to action. There is a discernible shift in values away from quantitative toward qualitative criteria for the good life. The nation's young people are responsible in large measure for this change in outlook. . . . The young well understand that we have gone beyond the point where environmental issues are limited to the protection of a stream, of a forest, or a stretch of shoreline. That protection is still needed, but it is no longer the central issue. The central issue is the health and welfare of man, wherever he lives, and whatever his station in life. It cuts across economic, social, and racial lines.

Young people also have developed to an art the ability to recognize the difference between form and substance. As a member of the Senate Subcommittee on Air and Water Pollution since 1967, I have experienced both. Having participated in the development of antipollution legislation at a time when there was only modest public interest in the problem, I was gratified when the president proclaimed in his state of the union message that he would propose "the most comprehensive and costly program in this field ever in the nation's history." He said "clean air, clean water, open spaces" should "once again be the birthright of every American."

He did not want to release the full $800 million appropriated for the grant program in fiscal 1969–70. He asked the Congress for $214 million, and that's all he wanted to spend. After being subjected to pressure from members of Congress and the general public, the White House relented and announced the full amount would be used.

The administration requested $106 million for the federal air pollution control program in fiscal 1970–71, nearly

$3 million less than the amount in the vetoed HEW appropriation bill. Congress appropriated $45 million for air pollution research in 1969–70, but the administration has requested only $27.9 million for fiscal 1970–71. For the solid-waste management program, $14.3 million was requested. This is identical to the appropriation for 1969–70, and the smallest request since 1966–67.

The White House announced in an executive order issued in early February that all projects or installations owned by or leased to the federal government must be designed, operated, and maintained as to comform to air and water quality standards by December 31, 1972. However, deficiencies need not be completed by that date—they only have to be under way by that date. Authority for granting extensions to the deadline was vested not in officials having jurisdiction over pollution control, but within the Bureau of the Budget. The date set in the order is six months beyond the deadline established by the Budget Bureau in 1967 for compliance with two executive orders on the subject issued in 1966.

According to a recent Harris survey, pollution control now ranks with aid to education at the top of the taxpayers' list of necessary federal funding. The president's assertion that the 1970s will be the environmental decade no doubt has spurred public interest in the subject. The president is to be commended for enlisting in the war on pollution, but in doing so he has set his sights too low in the financial commitment necessary to translate his prose into action.

If the administration feels it necessary to seek $290 million in fiscal '70–71 for development of a supersonic transport—a sum which incidentally represents an increase of more than 300 percent over the current appropriations—then surely it should reorder its priorities for environmental spending.

The interest generated by the teach-ins being held throughout the country hopefully will lead to a broad and responsible participation by young people in the political processes by which environmental policies are determined. If the crusade is to be successful, it must extend beyond the academic community. Everyone must be brought into the act. . . .

SENATOR SPONG is a Democrat from Virginia.

RICHARD L. OTTINGER

POLITICAL POLLUTION

Sarah Lawrence College, Bronxville, N.Y., April 22

It has been a long, hard fight to alert the public to the very real dangers that we face, I can well remember how difficult it was—only six years ago—to arouse public alarm over the appalling pollution of the Hudson River. I remember the general apathy when Consolidated Edison first proposed to deface the majestic Storm King Mountain at the gateway to the Hudson Highlands with a power plant. I can remember when people said that there was no way to keep the state of New York from dumping 9.5 million cubic yards of dirt into the Hudson to build a six-lane commercial expressway actually in the bed of that great river.

With each battle, more and more people have learned to cherish our environmental assets and to resist the destructive acts that threaten them. We are now making a slow start at cleaning up the Hudson; Con Edison's plant is still just a gleam in the greedy corporate eye, and the federal courts have told the governor that his expressway is a dead issue.

Unanimity raises the danger of a new kind of pollution —a form of pollution that may be the greatest threat of all—political pollution. It could undermine all the concern that has been focused and mobilized in this new movement.

When you find Nixon, Rockefeller, and Reagan on your side, you know you're in trouble. . . .

President Nixon said he was throwing $10 billion on the table "to put modern municipal waste treatment plants in every place in America where they are needed to make our waters clean again, and to do it now."

What a great promise!

But what are the facts?

When you read the small print, you find that only $4 billion of the pile on the table was to be federal money, the rest was to come from the states and localities. And we weren't exactly going to "do it now," the money is to be provided over the next five years, or maybe it was eight years. . . .

Furthermore, it is nothing but a dream that the local governments can come up with the 30 to 40 percent of multi-million-dollar sewage treatment projects that are required. It will just never happen. Apparently Mr. Nixon believes that big talk makes clean water. I won't accept that and I don't believe you will.

In his state of the state message this year, Governor Rockefeller promised a massive effort to protect the quality of our environment—an effort to be coordinated through a new agency to be known as the Department of Environmental Conservation.

But in his budget message to the New York State Legislature less than two weeks later, the governor proposed to increase expenditures for environmental problems by only $7 million, less than seven-tenths of 1 percent of the total budget monies he proposed. When it came to money, what were the real priorities? Take just one example: highways—one of the most effective environment destroyers. For highways the governor proposed to increase the budget by $42 million, *six times* the total increase for the environment.

In short, the Department of Environmental Conservation is just a new name painted on the same old door. When we open that door, we find the same tired faces, the same paralyzed bureaucracy, the same indifference to our predicament, and the same passion for erecting monuments at the expense of a ravaged environment. . . .

Five years ago, the people of New York State approved a billion-dollar pure-waters bond issue which, we were told, would clean up the waters of this state by 1970. In 1969, the governor asked the federal officials for a delay until 1972. Now there appears to be no firm date for completion of the cleanup. Instead, we have glowing reports of the success of the program—and just about the same amount of dirty water and dying rivers.

New York is by no means the only culprit. The problem

is national. Two months ago, I released to the public a report that was being carefully kept under wraps by the U. S. Army Corps of Engineers. This report revealed that years of dumping sewage sludge and dredge spoil into the ocean has created a foul Dead Sea barely twelve miles off the mouth of New York Harbor—a twenty-square-mile area incapable of supporting life and spreading rapidly toward our shores. Appalled by this ecological catastrophe and its obvious threat to our Atlantic fisheries and the beaches of New York and New Jersey, I called upon the President to stop the dumping at once so that we could halt the spread of this menace.

After two months of silence, we now have a bold new program. Just last week the president announced that we must, and I quote, "direct our attention to ocean dumping or we may court the same ecological damages that we have inflicted on our lands and inland waters."

And the action?

He called for a study to be made by the Council on Environmental Quality. . . .

The present rush for a seat on the environmental bandwagon is causing quite a clatter. Long-time conservationists are finding themselves in bed with some very strange fellows.

Let me give you this quote and then ask what head of what environmental protection agency said it: "We feel we've done a pretty good job in the environment aspects. Our people are proud of the water fowl flyways they've created, the growth of fishing, the care of ranges, the preservation of forests, the tremendous efforts in improving the quality of water. In fact, we feel we're in the forefront." End of quote. That statement, ladies and gentlemen, was made just last week by Lieutenant General Frederick J. Clarke, chief of that well-known conservation group, the Army Corps of Engineers, those wonderful folks who, among their other achievements, gave you the Dead Sea in New York Bight and an irrigation canal in the Florida Everglades which now threatens this rich natural asset with destruction.

If the list of our nation's outstanding conservationists now includes Richard Nixon and the corps of engineers, next thing you know, the President of Chevron Oil Company will be applying for membership in the Sierra Club.

There's another device down in Washington that is calculated to lull you to sleep while visions of federal billions dance in your head. This is known as the appropriations gap. As you know, legislation creating a new program in a given field such as, say air pollution control, includes a section *authorizing* the expenditure of a certain amount of money for the program. When such legislation is passed by Congress and signed by the president, we see headlines in our newspapers the next day proclaiming that: "New Clean Air Law Carries Billion-Dollar Price Tag." We may shake our heads a little about the cost, but it's good to know that the problem is finally being taken care of.

The joker in this hand is that the authorization is the amount that Congress *says* will be necessary to make this program work. Before any money appears, however, the administration must request legislation *appropriating* the money. And there's many a slip between the authorization and the appropriation.

For example, during the past five years, Congress has authorized more than $2.5 billion in federal grants for sewage treatment plants. It has cut that by more than one-third in the appropriation—a gap of a billion dollars. For air pollution control we have authorized about $550 million and appropriated about one-half, a gap of nearly a quarter of a billion dollars. Model Cities funds, which are intended to help eliminate one of the worst types of environmental pollution—unfit housing—show authorizations of nearly $2 billion and appropriations of about half that, a gap of a neat billion dollars.

Intense, incessant citizen pressure is the only thing that will save us. We must assume that we are surrounded by rapacious developers, callous industrialists, inept public agencies, and insensitive politicians, and our only salvation is in our own two hands. . . .

Make no mistake about it—this is a vitally important effort. One of our great scientists once pointed out that of all forms of life that have ever existed on this planet, 99 percent are now extinct—and to take literary license with the imperatives of evolutionary theory—they were *trying* to survive. The cold, hard facts is that they became extinct because, for various reasons, their environment could no longer support them. . . .

I believe all of us realize that the time for choosing is

upon us. We are nearly halfway through the first year of the last decade of life on Earth as we now know it. In this decade of the '70s, western civilization will choose one of two paths: it will stumble onto the path to extinction, or it will find the way to live in peace with nature and with itself.

REPRESENTATIVE OTTINGER is a Democrat from New York.

KURT VONNEGUT, JR.

NIXON'S THE ONE

Bryant Park, New York City, April 22

I have no idea which sporting event the president is watching this time of day. Perhaps a boxing match by satellite. I tell you this, that if we don't get our president's attention this planet may soon die. . . . He has our money and he has our power. He must use our money and power in order that the planet will not die. I am sorry he's a lawyer; I wish to God that he was a biologist. He said the other night that America has never lost a war, and he wasn't going to be the first American president to lose one. He may be the first American president to lose an entire planet.

He should help us make a fit place for human beings to live. Will he do it? No. So the war will go on. Meanwhile we go up and down Fifth Avenue picking up trash. . . .

KURT VONNEGUT is the author of *Cat's Cradle*, and, most recently, *Slaughterhouse-Five*.

President Nixon informally expressed approval of the Earth Day program but took no active part in it, spending a routine day in his White House office.

New York Times
April 23

Activities in Congress

April 22

Senate

Meets at noon on routine business.

Committees:

Appropriations Subcommittee—Office of Education. Commissioner James E. Allen. 10 a.m. Open. 1114 New Bldg.

Appropriations Subcommittee—D.C. 10 a.m. Open. 1225 New Bldg.

Interior—Montana power line. 9:30 a.m. Open. 3110 New Bldg.

Labor Special Subcommittee—NSF authorization. James Killian, George Kistiakowsky, Carl York, scientific advisers. 2 p.m. Open. 4232 New Bldg.

Post Office—Postal reorganization. 10 a.m. Open. 6202 New Bldg.

Appropriations Subcommittee—DOD: MUSMC. 10 p.m. Closed. S-126 Capitol.

Appropriations Subcommittee—Public works: AEC. 2 p.m. Closed. S-126 Capitol.

Aeronautical—Markup NASA. 2:30 p.m. Closed. 235 Old Bldg.

Judiciary—Committee business. 10:30 a.m. Closed. 2300 New Bldg.

Conferees—D.C. crime. 2 p.m. Closed. S-228 Capitol.

House

Meets at noon on space authorization bill.

Committees:

Agriculture—Continue on general farm legislation—10 a.m., closed 1301 Longworth Bldg.

Armed Services—Subcommittee No. 4, on miscellaneous bills, members Congress and department witnesses—10 a.m., open 2212 Rayburn Bldg.

Armed Services—My Lai incident subcommittee, military personnel Maj. Charles C. Calhoun, Maj. Frederick W. Watke, Lt. Col. John L. Holladay, and Brig. Gen. George H. Young—10 a.m., closed 2339 Rayburn Bldg.

Education and Labor—Select subcommittee on labor, continue on manpower legislation, witnesses, E. B. Whitten, Natl. Rehabilitation Assn., Washington; Walter C. Helms, Jr., Fairfax, Va., accompanied by Dr. John Walsh, president William Hood, Dunwoodie Industry, institutes of Minneapolis; Dr. Arthur Lee, president-elect, Phoenix, Ariz., Dr. Hirsch, San Francisco; and Markham Ball, Health and Welfare Council of the National Capital Area—9:30 a.m., open 2175 Rayburn Bldg.

Education and Labor—Gen. subcommittee on labor, continue on private welfare and pension plan legislation. I. W. Abel, president United Steelworkers of America—10 a.m. open 2257 Rayburn Bldg.

Foreign Affairs—Subcommittee on international organizations and movements, H. J. Res. 1146—Grant, expand U.N. headquarters, witnesses, Samuel de Palma, asst. secy. for international organization affairs, State Department, and Charles W. Yost, U.S. representative to U.N.—10 a.m., open 2200 Rayburn Bldg.

Interior—Subcommittees on national parks and recreation mark-up HR 555-Apostle Islands national seashore and HR 14114—Improve administration of national park system—9:45 a.m., closed 1329 Longworth Bldg.

Commerce—Subcommittee on transportation and aeronautics. HR 7068—Federal Railroad Safety Act. John H. Reed, chairman National Transportation Safety Board—10 a.m., open 2123 Rayburn Bldg.

Judiciary—Subcommittee, No. 5, (antitrust). Continue on conglomerate mergers. Continue hearing reps. of Ling-Temco-Vought Inc. Witnesses, James J. Ling, chief executive officer; Clyde Skeen, president, and George E. Griffin, vice president–financial plans —10 a.m., open 2141 Rayburn Bldg.

Merchant Marine—HR 15424—New maritime program—10 a.m., closed 1334 Longworth Bldg.

Post Office—Continue on postal reform. George Meany, president, AFL-CIO—10 a.m., open 210 Cannon Bldg.

Public Works—Subcommittee on roads. Continue on highway legislation. Public witnesses—10 a.m., open 2167 Rayburn Bldg.

Public Works—Subcommittee on public buildings and grounds. Pending business—11:45 a.m., closed 2167 Rayburn Bldg.

Public Works—Pending business—11:45 a.m., closed 2167 Rayburn Bldg.

Rules—On pending business—10:30 a.m., closed H-313 Capitol.

Ways and Means—Continue on Social Security—10 a.m., closed Committee Room Longworth Bldg.

Commerce—Subcommittee on public health and welfare. Drug abuse legislation—10 a.m., closed 2322 Rayburn Bldg.

Appropriations — Subcommittees: Pub. Works, H-307; Transportation, H-236; Defense, H-140; Labor-HEW, H-164; Foreign Operations (1:00 p.m.), H-309, D.C. (1:30 p.m.), H-302—10 a.m., closed.

PART III

GREEN REVOLUTION

The rich and powerful are killing all the butterflies. If your children are to see butterflies you must be a revolutionary and yourself take control of your life and its surroundings.

—Anonymous

ERIC SEVAREID

BEYOND EARTH DAY

CBS Evening News with Walter Cronkite
7:00–7:30 P.M. (EST), April 22

Earth Day will have to be extended to Earth Year, Decade, Generation if the poisoning of water, air, and soil is to be halted or even appreciably slowed down. The issue is of that dimension. This exercise is not to be confused with community paint-up, clean-up weeks coincident with the first nice days of spring.

It seems a fair guess that pollution will not only continue indefinitely as a prime public issue, but that it will become intensely controversial, on the federal level with fights over budgets and agency powers, and even more unfriendly on local levels where specific factories, products, practices, and plots of land and bodies of water are concerned. Almost anywhere that some advance is made for the general public, some specific individuals are going to lose something. In the end, presumably, everybody will have to pay for the transition; the quarrels will be over how the burdens are to be shared.

The issue will be front and center for at least the rest of the twentieth century. Pollution goes hand in hand not only with population growth but with the growth of industry, and neither population nor industry is about to stop growing. With some other issues, like poverty or equality or economic and educational opportunity, the main current seems to be forward in spite of many back eddies; in the matter of pollution the main current is backward in spite of many forward eddies.

We are now dealing with final facts, the chemistry and physics of plant and animal existence, not with the metaphysics of freedom, justice, equality, or the other elastic elements in human happiness.

Americans have a world reputation as the people with a reverence for the facts and the figures, the people of the know-how, if not always the know-why. This is the big test of the knowhow and this time we do know-why.

ERIC SEVAREID is a TV news commentator and writer.

JAMES B. PEARSON

ANTIPOLLUTION AND WARM PUPPIES

By Telephone
Kansas Wesleyan University, Salina, Kans., April 22

I want to warn that antipollution is not what we politicians call a "warm puppy" issue, one which if we pass enough laws, spend enough money and have a good heart, happiness is assured and soon America will be beautiful again. Antipollution means that someone will be hurt. Profits must be cut, comforts reduced, taxes raised, sacrifices endured. And, as in all human struggles, the powerful will fight the hardest to be hurt the least.

SENATOR PEARSON is a Republican from Kansas.

CHANNING E. PHILLIPS

Unity

Sylvan Theater, Washington, D.C., April 22

We are here tonight to pay tribute to life—the kind of life we would like to live, in the kind of environment we would like to have.

We are here tonight because mankind, in his own ferocious quest to extract every drop of economic lifeblood from the Earth, has created for himself a monstrous septic tank in which he must now live.

And we are here tonight because man has begun to realize that he must do something before he chokes to death in his own garbage.

The statistics and illustrations are legion—from the unhatched pelicans of California to the oil-soaked ducks of the East Coast; from the mine-scarred strips of West Virginia to the concrete and asphalt highways of the metropolis; from the beer-can litter of the passing auto to the automobile graveyards in our cities' alleys. Land, water, air, people, birds, fish, animals—all are caught up in the stench of sickness and death whose proportions now threaten man's survival. It is not an occasion for panic; it is an occasion for deep concern. Black people who have lived in this filth for decades can tell you that man can live in far worse environments than you think. Rats and roaches, flaking lead paint and industrial waste, filthy air and auto-clogged streets—these are standard appointments in the inner city, the white man's bequest to the inner-city blacks. But now that White America is being threatened, perhaps we can deal with black needs and white needs—human needs—in a united effort to remedy the value system that has brought us to this Earth Day.

. . . Yet our emphasis is on expanded production; and

as we sail on to higher and higher Gross National Products, we create human and other flotsam and jetsam for which our system holds little responsibility.

We take pride in America because we produce more short tons of cotton and more tin cans than any other country in the world; but we also lead the league in the production of industrial waste.

We take pride in America because we have a higher standard of living than does any other country in the world; but tend to overlook the fact that over 40 million Americans stand well below that standard of living. And averaging out doesn't lessen the hunger and deprivation of those 40 million.

In the good old puritan tradition we have taken the book of Genesis seriously and set out to subdue the Earth, and to have dominion over all things. And in two hundred years we have subdued it with asphalt, DDT, and industrial waste. But some of our leaders seem to think that it is the will of God, and if you tend not to believe it, then you can check the GNP.

And so we are here tonight—April 22, 1970—to celebrate something called Earth Day, in the midst of Enviornment Week, to pledge ourselves and our energies to undoing what we have done, or at the very least, to stop doing it as rapidly. The problems are real, our concern is legitimate, and we are here in good faith.

There has been some talk about this concern for the environment being a diversionary tactic of the administration to defuse the dissent against war and racial injustice. I wouldn't be surprised. But I'm here tonight not because we're changing issues in the middle of the stream, but out of a deep conviction that racial injustice, war, urban blight, and environmental rape have a common denominator in our exploitative economic system. And that as you pursue your legitimate concern with the pollution of our environment, you will discover that our basic problem is pollution of the mind—a value system that uses the profit motive not as fuel which moves us along, but as the compass that determines our direction. Priorities are determined not by need, but by profit.

Some of you may know of the Project for Corporate Responsibility launched by Ralph Nader, which is mounting Campaign GM. We are asking for certain kinds of interests to be included in the board of directors of General Motors—consumer interests, minority interests, and environmental interests—interests not likely to be included in our nation's corporate structures through the normal method of choosing directors based on their ability to increase profits or the size of their stock-biddings. That also is a part of the picture that brings us here tonight.

Racism is a fact of our national life only because in the search for cheap labor, slavery and racism increased profits.

Urban blight is a fact of our national life only because it is more profitable to relocate than to rehabilitate.

War is a fact of our national life only because short-term profits and maximum control of resources and markets are more visible than long-term retaliation from an economically or politically oppressed people.

And environmental rape is a fact of our national life only because it is more profitable than responsible stewardship of Earth's limited resources.

So that is why I join you tonight—not only because you are convinced that pollution is a pressing problem, but because I am convinced that the solution to your problem will also help solve the black man's problem, confined as he is in urban squalor—or to use your language, environmental pollution.

As we pursue this cause we must make sure our priorities are more just than those we fight.

> The immediate environment a man lives in twenty four hours a day is more important than the waters he fishes in on weekends:
>
> The trees and green spaces and beauties of nature can be a nightmare to the man who has no protection from the elements—a home!;
>
> The extermination of rats and vermin by the rehabilitation of our cities is more important than the disappearance of the brown pelican.

So do your thing so well that those who might have raised or supported this issue as a diversionary tactic will discover that in fact they have opened a Pandora's box in their own eyes—but a medicine chest in the eyes of all who "seek a newer world," the decent and humane society where men live in harmony with each other and with nature.

I end, as I began, with the conviction that there is a common denominator to our concerns and a mutuality in our efforts, that the problems that confront us in seemingly separate ways are in fact seriously interwoven. It is stated beautifully in the New Haggadah for Passover, and the fact that a black man would point to these words is a symbol of the unity we must find to accomplish the humane life:

> For if we were to end a single genocide but not to stop the other wars that are killing men and women as we sit here, it would not be sufficient;
>
> If we were to end those bloody wars but not disarm the nations of the weapons that could destroy all Mankind, it would not be sufficient;
>
> If we were to disarm the nations but not to end the pollution and poisoning of our planet, it would not be sufficient;
>
> If we were to end the poisoning of our planet but not prevent some people from wallowing in luxury while others starved, it would not be sufficient;
>
> If we were to make sure that no one starved but not to end police brutality in many countries, it would not be sufficient;
>
> If we were to end outright police brutality but not to free the daring poets from their jails, it would not be sufficient;
>
> If we were to free the poets from their jails but to cramp the minds of people so that they could not understand the poets, it would not be sufficient;
>
> If we liberated all men and women to understand the free creative poets but forbade them to explore their own inner ecstasies, it would not be sufficient;
>
> If we allowed men and women to explore their inner ecstasies but would not allow them to love one another and share in the human fraternity, it would not be sufficient.
>
> How much then are we in duty bound to struggle, work, share, give, think, plan, feel, organize, sit-in, speak out, dream, hope, and be on behalf of Mankind! For we must end the genocide (in Vietnam), stop the bloody wars that are killing men and women as we sit here, disarm the nations of the deadly weapons that threaten to destroy us all, end the poisoning of our planet, make sure that no one starves, stop police brutality in many countries, free the poets from their jails, educate us all to understand their

poetry, liberate us all to explore our inner ecstasies, and encourage and aid us to love one another and share in the human fraternity. All these!

The REVEREND CHANNING PHILLIPS is president of the Housing and Development Corporation of Washington, D.C., and a Campaign GM nominee for the board of directors of General Motors.

HARRIET MILLER

Getting Oil Out

San Fernando Valley State College
Los Angeles, Calif., April 22

We're stuck with oil in Santa Barbara. We're going to stick with this fight. I hope you do too—and that Earth Day isn't just a one-day stand. . . .

The granting of leases for oil development in the Santa Barbara Channel was one small incident in a long pattern of exploitation of our resources. What happened was not unusual. It was usual. Despite the protests of many Santa Barbarans, the government in 1968 sold seventy-one leases to oil companies for the attractive sum of over $600-million. Six hundred million dollars won over the lives of birds and seals; it won over beautiful beaches and an exquisite ocean view. Six hundred million dollars won because that is like it is. The big interests, the moneyed interests, the powerful interests got their way because that is the way our system traditionally has operated. Isn't "progress" good for the country? Isn't oil development "progress?"

The Santa Barbara disaster that occurred when the well blew out on January 28, 1969, perhaps helped to bring into focus the nation's environmental crisis. The oil disaster —along with other tragedies—became a symbol of what has been happening, and what is happening at an accelerated pace, and what threatens all of us unless this trend toward economic exploitation at any cost can at least be slowed down.

The fact that drilling continues in the Santa Barbara Channel should not surprise anyone. The weight of tradition, not to mention money, is on the side of oil development. . . .

We want those drilling platforms out of the channel. We

live with the constant threat of another major blowout. And, despite our past failures, or even because of them, there are a lot of people who won't give up until every last platform is out of the Santa Barbara Channel.

But this particular battle may take a long time because it isn't easy to reverse what has happened. It is much easier to prevent it from happening another time, now that people are aware, and vigilant, and recognize what kind of action has to be taken in advance. . . .

Until an approach acceptable to the companies and the Congress is successful, drilling and oil production will continue in the Santa Barbara Channel despite the protests, petitions, fish-ins, or what-have-you. It is that simple. And the prospects are anything but encouraging. Recently it was pointed out that as many as 960 new oil wells could be drilling under permits already approved by the Interior Department.

We in Santa Barbara believe our tragedy has helped to turn the tide of public opinion. We can only hope that action will come fast enough to save the channel and to prevent similar exploitation from occurring elsewhere. Whether this happens or not depends on each and every one of us and our commitment to make this land a better place to live.

HARRIET MILLER is a member of the board of directors of Get Oil Out (GOO), Inc., Santa Barbara, Calif.

GEORGE WALD

Environmental Traps

Harvard University, Cambridge, Mass., April 21

I wonder whether it's by design that Earth Day comes at Passover. Only this year one ought to celebrate Passover in reverse. It's we who are being subjected to the ten plagues and the first of those plagues was water pollution.

I have been so interested in all the things that were said, I have made notes all through this meeting for speech after speech, but there's no time for even one of them. It's time for *you* to begin to speak.

And yet I'd like to assure Senator Muskie we know more about that stuff in outer space than perhaps he realizes. And there's nothing in the entire remainder of the solar system as precious as one acre on the Earth. I'm terribly glad that we got those three astronauts back. Thank heavens for that. There's only one thing to add. They shouldn't have gone.

The environment has been called a motherhood issue. Everybody's for motherhood, though one can get even too much of that. And it's easy to hold eloquent speeches about it, but there comes the point at which one has to decide what to do. And then one finds that one is encountering very powerful forces, both powerful and sensitive. Mr. Nixon has come into this discussion before. He's for the environment too. I shall never forget reading of that day when Mr. Nixon, walking with his good friend Bebe Rebozo over his real-estate options in San Clemente, said, "Bebe, we'll have to keep it this way." And that brought him into the environment movement.

A lot of harsh things have been said about technology. Technology can be very useful. It all depends on the way it's used. Technology is the application of science to useful ends. In any properly conducted society, all technology new and old should be under constant review in terms of the needs and goals and aspirations of society. And who is to make those judgments—for one of our troubles now is that those decisions are all being made by the producers of technology. One should listen to them and all they have to say. But in any properly conducted society, the ultimate decision should be made not by the producers, but by those who will have to live with the product.

I think that our new concern with the environment represents a dominant issue. It will go on, because it has to. One has no choice. It puts one up against problems so difficult that if one could only avoid them, it would be wise to do so, but one can't. We're not being *asked* to take care of the environment; we're being *told*.

There are two traps concealed in the whole business. Both of them have been mentioned before tonight. Let me say them again. One can hardly say them too often. The first of them is—we mustn't let the environment and a concern with pollution become a distraction from our other issues: the Vietnam war; the draft; the size of our military budget; indeed the militarization of our country. We'll have to take care of the environment and take care of all those other things too.

The second trap is even more insidious. And there are powerful forces promoting both these traps. That second trap would be to let antipollution become our new multibillion-dollar business: to let the pollution go on merrily in all its present forms, and superimpose a new multibillion-dollar business of antipollution on top of it. And in these days of conglomerates, it would be the same business. One branch of it would be polluting, the other branch of it antipolluting.

And so there's only one way of coping with this situation reasonably, and that is to attack it at its source. And immediately one runs into these extraordinarily powerful forces. The biggest polluter in the country is the automobile and so one has the automobile industry on one's hands, and the oil industry along with it. We need fewer cars on the roads. And much better public transportation.

All these things are very closely interrelated. After the auto industry as a polluter, we have a lot of other powerful forces to deal with. The lumber industry—a big polluter.

The power industry—a tremendous polluter; and all terribly powerful. So we are going to have a job on our hands, and yet that's the way it has to be done, if it's ever to work. If it's ever to make any sense, we'll have to cut pollution at its source.

You know, as I listen to professors in other fields as well as my own, I hear over and over again something that I've come to think of as the *rational fallacy,* the fallacy that consists in somehow picturing this as a reasonable world full of concerned people who are doing their best for us all. I was very interested to hear from Professor Levitt that our industry is primarily concerned with raising our standard of living. It's a curious idea. . . .

All the militant kids go about shaking their heads off about something they call imperialism. Well, imperialism is very serious business in the world today. Oil is a fine example of its operation. But imperialism is a little old-fashioned, and it's peanuts compared to the big game. And that's what I'd like to talk about.

That big game is sometimes called domestic imperialism, but I like better Juan Bosch's name for it. Juan Bosch is the ex-president of the Dominican Republic who would be its present president if Mr. Johnson hadn't sent in the marines. So Juan Bosch has a name for it. He calls it Pentagonism. I'd like to tell you about it in my own way.

The other day I looked up the Gross National Product of South Vietnam. You know more or less what a Gross National Product is—it's just everything that passes hands in the course of a year. The year was 1968. It's all the production, all the trading, all that passed hands in the course of the year 1968 in South Vietnam. How much do you suppose it was? $2.5 billion. Peanuts.

You see, if you moved into South Vietnam as good old-fashioned imperialists and wrung it dry, you could get yourself a cut of $2.5 billion. It isn't worth bothering with. We're spending $30 billion a year on that war over there, and a good friend who is nearby and who was President Eisenhower's science advisor tells me that as well as he can figure it, we've got $20 billion worth of military hardware over there right now.

That got me sort of interested and I looked up the Gross National Product of the whole of southeast Asia.

Five nations—North Vietnam, South Vietnam, Laos,

Cambodia, and Thailand—80 million people. In 1968 the Gross National Product for those five nations was $11.3 billion. Peanuts.

The ABM program alone in its present thin, Safeguard form is worth $12 billion. The MIRV program that's just getting started is worth an estimated $17 billion. And the sales of General Motors in the same year, 1968, $22-some-odd billion—twice the Gross National Product of the whole of South Vietnam, and the whole livelihood of 80 million people.

That's a private enterprise. It's being managed well. It has told us over the years not to look on it as a private concern—to look on it, on the contrary, as a national enterprise. You all know what "Engine Charlie" Wilson said—"What's good for General Motors is good for the nation." And there are all those hundreds of thousands of shareholders, all good Americans, participating in running General Motors.

Until Mr. Nader and his raiders turn up. And then it turns out that the last thing in the world that shareholders are to do is to vote against management. Our Harvard Corporation is taking an awfully long time to make up its mind to vote our 280-odd-thousand shares in the public interest. It isn't at all clear that General Motors would make any less money. Those are pretty innocuous suggestions that Nader has made for adding to the General Motors articles of incorporation, but there's that "faith in management."

As I read in *Newsweek*, General Motors' attitude with regard to those two proposals to be added to the articles of incorporation in the public interest is—they are going to do it, but they're asking the shareholders to vote against them. That's to show confidence in management. One wonders how far it goes. The sales of General Motors in a year are bigger than the Gross National Products of all but a few nations on the earth. One wonders how far confidence in management is to go. How about the voters laying off and letting government manage without voter interference?

You may think I'm talking off the subject. No, not at all. General Motors makes more than half the cars in the country, and hence it has the proud position, I rather think, of being the biggest single polluter in the country.

So I think we have our problems. I think one of the things we really have to deal with is the degraded view of the American as *consumer*. I've just told you about Pentagonism: let me go on a bit. . . .

You see, the whole point of that situation I began to describe to you is that if that's the kind of money you want to make, those multibillion-dollar contracts that lately took the place of multimillion-dollar contracts—if you want to make that kind of money, you have to go where it is. You can't make that kind of money out of southeast Asians—they don't have it. You can't make it out of Africans—they don't have it. You can't make it out of South Americans—they don't have it.

If you want to make that kind of money, you have to go where it is. And where is that? That's we. We have it. And when Professor Levitt suggests that we fix up pollution with big taxes, there are people who pay taxes, and there are a lot fewer people who receive those taxes. You can't solve the situation just with taxation. Taxation is the very means by which this particular system—Pentagonism—operates.

And that's the hang-up. It's the American, not as man and woman, but as consumer. The primary duty of every good American is to consume his share. That's why most of my generation are so incensed with the hippie style. The hippies have some troubles, but most of them are their own private business. But there's one trouble with hippies that cuts at the roots of American life—*they don't consume enough*. Not enough clothes, not enough haircuts, not enough expensive food, not enough high-rental properties. And that's the hang-up.

And I think this environmental concern now that brings us here tonight, and our concern with the war, and our concern with the draft, and our concern with the militarization of the country, and our concern with Pentagonism—they are all interrelated. What we have to begin to do is to repossess America. By repossessing America, we'll repossess our common humanity. The American as a human being. With clean air to breathe. With decent water to drink that fish would accept—they don't accept the water we drink now. With grass to walk on—grass is frightfully important. . . .

To live a decent human life, you need those intangibles—clean air, clean water, grass—who can eat grass? You need it just the same. Trees, relationship to animals. Sounds sentimental doesn't it? You forget those things and you're just a fraction of a man. And that's what we are out to do—to try to become whole men and women again.

GEORGE WALD is professor of biology at Harvard University and a corecipient of the 1967 Nobel Prize in physiology and medicine.

ANDREW GARLING

THE MOVEMENT

Bryant Park, New York City, April 22

As groups were organizing around the country for this day, they weren't mounting a national antismog campaign or a clean-up-the-rivers day. They were building for a movement to start testing what's around them, to face the reality of what's ahead if we keep on as we have in this country. . . .

As people were zeroing in on their local environmental problems, they were realizing that some supporting pillars in our complex society were put together in a fundamentally wrong way.

We're going to the courts, going to the polls, going to stockholders' meetings, and going to the streets.

This movement is going to start turning things around.

What is good for General Motors, what is good for the Interior Department–oil industry–highway builders' complex, and what is good for the Pentagon turns out to be pretty rough on the rest of us.

ANDREW GARLING is northeast coordinator for Environmental Action.

JOSEPH SHAPIRO

Imperialism

Fordham University, New York City, April 22

. . . I do believe that a politically effective ecological movement can develop. It will be radical in nature because the solutions of the problems require revolutionary changes in social, economic, and political institutions. To be effective, this movement cannot work in isolation; it must relate itself to other social and political problems afflicting our society.

The Vietnam war and the ecological crisis have the same roots. Both are products of a highly technological, mechanistic, dehumanized society; in the one case ruthlessly expanding its interests in southeast Asia, in the other, ruthlessly expanding its interests at home; in the one case economic imperialism; in the other, ecological imperialism. One can't fight one without fighting the other.

Joseph Shapiro is an associate professor of physics at Fordham University in New York City.

RENNIE DAVIS

Up Agnew Country

Sylvan Theater, Washington, D. C., April 22

The jury in Chicago said we were not guilty of conspiracy. But if there was no conspiracy in Chicago, there sure as hell is now.

Yes, it's official—the conspiracy against pollution. And we have a simple program—arrest Agnew and smash capitalism. We make only one exception to our pollution stand—everyone should light up a joint and get stoned.

We gather tonight in the headquarters for Agnew country. Tonight Agnew is thinking he's got us running around the country, picking up garbage, getting ourselves into peaceful rallies to demonstrate our impressive numbers, to prove our nonviolence. It took us five years, exactly five years, to learn the lesson in Chicago that whites as well as blacks will find that channels in this country are dead-end streets where people get clubbed, maced or ignored trying to work through the "system" on a single issue.

So we say to Agnew country that we are not going to be tricked into an ecology movement that diverts us from our revolutionary purposes. We say tonight that we are an ecology movement that intends to join forces with the people who have taken to the streets of this country in the demand to end the genocide in Southeast Asia.

We are an ecology movement that is integral with those who say "black liberation now." We tell Richard Nixon that ecology to us means going to New Haven to stop the electrocution of Bobby Seale and to free the New Haven 9. We are an ecology movement that must support and work for the demands of the most oppressed class of people in this country—women. Let Nixon know that this is our perspective: an end to a system based on the prerogatives of private greed rather than social need.

When I was in Hanoi in 1967 I met a woman—an old woman sixty-five or seventy years old—who was bent over a broom, sweeping a street in the city of Hanoi. I told her that of all the cities that I had been in, that the streets of Hanoi were among the cleanest anywhere in the world. And that woman turned to me, and she said, "Hanoi used to be a city that was filled with garbage and dirt and prostitutes, but now every day, I can show the people of this city what it means to have freedom and independence."

What we are saying is that we are going to pick up the shit in this country, but in the context of a movement to liberate ourselves. We are saying "No" to the leadership that wants to use us as tools for liberal politicians. We are saying that we will not be co-opted for token changes in a system that plunders and rapes and destroys all over the world. We say to Agnew country that Earth Day is for the sons and daughters of the American Revolution who are going to tear this capitalism down and set us free.

RENNIE DAVIS is a member of the Chicago Seven.

CLIFFORD P. CASE

On in Freedom

Seven New Jersey Colleges, April 22

. . . We are no longer able to rely upon our institutions to prevent the disruption of our life in these and other ways. Our laws and institutions are under attack. They have been challenged and defied, though clothed in the majesty of government itself, when they ignored the legitimate grievances of any group in our society. . . .

We can build a police state so strong and so ruthlessly repressive that no disrupting protest can be made. With modern technology such repression could be complete and more horrible than any known before. . . .

Or we can decide to go on in freedom. But if we make this choice, we must realize that we can't do it in the old way. Justified complaints and grievances, even of relatively small minorities, can no longer be indefinitely ignored. We've got to make a decent effort to meet them or face the pulling down of the pillars which support the ever more intricate structure of modern civilization. . . .

What have justice and freedom to do with the environment?

The answer is: Everything. At least that's the answer for me.

Bare survival would be a poor thing indeed if it were survival in a world without justice and without freedom.

Senator Case is a Republican from New Jersey.

EDMUND S. MUSKIE

A WHOLE SOCIETY

Harvard University and University of Pennsylvania Cambridge, Mass., and Philadelphia, Pa., April 21–22

. . . First, I want to define for you what I think the environmental crisis means.

It means that we must outgrow our traditional way of solving problems one at a time—each in its own limited context—and unrelated to side effects.

It means that we must rethink what we mean by "cost," what is economical or not economical, or what we can afford or cannot afford to do.

It means, at bottom, that our old value systems—whatever may be said for or against them—no longer respond to our needs or fit goals relevant to our future.

Those who believe that the environmental crisis relates to trees and not people are wrong.

Those who believe that we are talking about the Grand Canyon and the Catskills, but not Harlem and Watts are wrong.

And those who believe that we must do something about the SST and the automobile, but not ABMs and the Vietnam War are wrong. . . .

Our goal has never been to create a society where human greatness took a back seat to economic growth and technological change. We have sought a society where men could live in harmony with their environment and in peace with each other. In many respects, our growing economy and our mushrooming technology have moved us toward that goal. But in too many other ways, the costs of unrestrained and uncontrolled growth have caught up with us.

If economic growth means rivers that are fire hazards, we had better redirect economic growth.

If prosperity means children dying from lead poisoning, we had better redistribute prosperity.

And if progress means technology that produces more kinds of things than we really want, more kinds of things than we really need and more kinds of things than we can live with, we had better redefine progress.

We are not powerless to effect these changes.

We must go to the ballot box with an environmental conscience and elect leaders who have made a commitment to a healthy total environment.

We must go to stockholders' meetings with the power of proxies, as Campaign GM seeks to do, and require industries to change their ways of doing business.

And we must go to the cash register with the power of our dollars and buy from industries that do not pollute.

If one phrase can characterize our traditional outlook as Americans, that phrase has been, "There's more where that came from."

We have thought that there was always more of everything. But now the time is coming—or it is here—when there is no more:

— no more clean air or clean water;
— no more room for our garbage and trash;
— no more patience for poverty; and,
— no more tolerance for energy-sapping wars, overseas or at home. Whether or not we can find ways to achieve fundamental change in a free society is the acid test of a democratic experiment.

The environmental conscience may be the way to turn the nation around. All we need is hardheaded decisions to save our own skins. . . .

Our technology has reached a point where it is producing more kinds of things than we really want, more kinds of things than we really need, and more kinds of things than we can really live with.

We have to choose, to say no, and to give up some luxuries. And these kinds of decisions will be the acid test of our commitment to a healthy environment.

It means choosing cleaner cars rather than faster cars, more parks instead of more highways, and more houses and more schools instead of more weapons and more wars.

The whole society that we seek is one in which all men live in brotherhood with each other and with their environment. It is a society where each member of it knows that he has an opportunity to fulfill his greatest potential.

It is a society that will not tolerate slums for some and decent houses for others, rats for some and playgrounds for others, clean air for some and filth for others.

It is the only kind of society that has a chance. It is the only kind of society that has a future.

To achieve a whole society—a healthy total environment—we need change, planning more effective and just laws and more money better spent.

Achieving that whole society will cost heavily—in foregone luxuries, in restricted choices, in higher prices for certain goods and services, in taxes, and in hard decisions about our national priorities. It will require a new sense of balance in our national commitments. . . .

The only strategy that makes sense is a total strategy to protect the total environment.

The only way to achieve that total strategy is through an Environmental Revolution—a commitment to a whole society.

The Environmental Revolution must be one of laws, not men; one of values, not ideology; and one of achievement, not unfulfilled promises.

We are not powerless to accomplish this change, but we are powerless as a people if we wait for someone else to do it for us.

We can use the power of the people to turn the nation around—to move toward a whole society. . . .

SENATOR MUSKIE is a Democrat from Maine.

PART IV

BLACK SURVIVAL

Interviewer: What are doing about air pollution?
Passerby: Well, I ain't breathin' too hard.

—Man-on-the-Street Television Interview
Washington, D.C.

FREDDIE MAE BROWN AND THE ST. LOUIS METROPOLITAN BLACK SURVIVAL COMMITTEE

Black Survival: A Collage of Skits

Page-Park YMCA and Lincoln High, St. Louis, Mo.
6:30 and 8:30 P.M. (CST), April 22

. . . This collage of skits emphasizes the amount of pollution we live in and makes you more aware (we hope) of how detrimental such an environment is to the health of you, me, and our loved ones. The intricate biological life scheme of the world is being destroyed more rapidly with each year that passes, and soon, if this destruction is not stopped, every living thing on the face of the Earth will die. . . .

Scene 1: Boy and girl in the house talking. Father keeps walking through the room. The couple gets uncomfortable.

Girl: Let's go outside and sit on the porch. It's getting stuffy in here.

(They go outside and immediately begin to cough)

Boy: I think we better go back in, we can at least breathe inside.

(Lights slowly dim) . . .

* * *

Scene 2: The setting is at the entrance of a college building. Four students have just finished their final examinations. They are overjoyed to be going on a two-week spring break. Outside the building a professor who is known and respected by the four students is preparing to demonstrate against environmental pollution.

Jan: Boy, am I glad those final examinations are over. This last one was a monster!

Will: This two-week spring break is right on time. I sure can use this time to relax my brains.

James: What brains? If you really had brains, man, you would really be dangerous. But I must agree I can certainly use the two-week rest.

Ruth: Am I going to use up some of this good spring weather? The flowers, grass, trees, and the whole bit.

Debby: There's Professor Wilson. I wonder what he's up to now.

James: What's happening, prof? Aren't you going to stop work long enough to enjoy the spring break?

Professor Wilson: I would like to but I have the task of organizing a movement against the environmental ills in the black neighborhoods. Can I get you students involved?

Will: Not me, prof, I would rather spend my time doing something that will *help* my black brothers such as getting them jobs, education, and housing. (Ball up fist and raise it high)

Professor: Well, let me explain what this movement is all about.

Will: No, I heard about the movement for a better environment and I feel like it's a cop-out from dealing with the real problems which are education and employment. No, that just ain't my bag. I let you and whitey take care of that.

(GROUP WALKS AWAY———)

Debby: I'm surprised at Professor Wilson get involved in something like air pollution.

James: Yes, 'cause I always thought he was a mellow fellow.

Ruth: Me too, because he was such a big help to the Black Student Association when they made their demands to the administration last spring.

Will: I really hated to turn him off the way I did, but I can't dig that air pollution bag. It seems like more of a white mothers' club thing to me.

Debby: Well, different strokes for different folks.

(GROUP TENDS TO MOVE WITH THE MUSIC ON THE RADIO (TAPE RECORDS)

Ruth: I really like that record, they tell me it's number one back home.

James: Speaking of home—when are you leaving, Ruth? I hope you can come to our set tomorrow night.

Ruth: The fact is I'm not going home. I be right here, doing the break. I thought it would be nice to stay here in Pleasantville and get the full worth of spring for a change. You see, I live in the city and not such a good part at that. Spring there is no different than any other time of the year. Everything is so dull and dreary—there are no flowers, trees, and grass. There are even no birds to sing. But then who could blame them for not wanting to live in that neighborhood. We're crazy to live there ourselves.

Debby: Say, girl, I'm glad you are staying here because I'm staying too. I thought it would be great to have my parents come up to visit me. You see my neighborhood is very very similar to yours and my folks never get to take a vacation. Can you imagine having to stay in a setting like ours at home for years without a break? Anyway, I felt that they would really enjoy the spring up here.

James: Since both of you girls are going to be on campus then both of you are invited to our party. And maybe we can plan something for the rest of the spring break.

Debby: You're not going home (to James).

James: No, you know I have this asthmatic condition. It doesn't bother me too much up here in Pleasantville where the air is clean but back home in the city I suffer all the time. So I'm staying with the fresh air.

Will: Well, I'm staying here too and I don't have asthma. And I don't particularly get turned on by the flowers and birds—to tell it like it is I don't like the slums and want to be there as little as possible.

(PAUSE)

You know what we have all said? We have said that we hate to go home because our home areas are not fit to live in. It's good to be able to make that choice. But what about the people who live there daily and don't have a choice? People like Debbie's parents or my folks. I just told Prof Wilson that I would rather fight for jobs and education for black people and then they can move out of that kind of environment. But after the jobs and education there are still going to be those who can't leave. My mother and father, my aunt Mary, Uncle Joe, my grandmother, and thousands of others who don't get jobs or education. What do we do about these people?

Ruth: There are government programs such as medicare and rent supplement programs that will help them.

Will: Yes, but are these programs working?

James: To answer that very simply—no. They are not—and personally I don't think they will ever work or that they were designed to work. The point that I think you are trying to make is, "What can we do about the problem?"

Will: This is exactly what I'm saying. It seems to me that our efforts to better the black conditions have been too narrow to help all the people. Sure some will get jobs and open doors for others to get work but this does not seem to satisfy all the needs. I think we must begin to fight all the problems that make for our slum environment. Even air pollution! It is much too important to leave it for whitey to solve for us.

Debby: Yes, because I'm getting so that I don't trust whitey to commit himself fully to black problems. I'd like to be around to see that we get all that's coming to us.

Ruth: Maybe we should go back and talk to Prof Wilson and see what his program is all about.

ALL: Yes, let's do—mellow. (BOYS HIT HANDS)

James: Prof, we have come back to reconsider your offer if it is designed to help the black brother. Tell us about it.

Prof.: Well, we are trying to do a couple of things. We would first like to inform the black community about some of the environmental insults that are unique to the black area and of some of the forces that created and maintained the conditions. Secondly, we would like to tell the white community our definitions of environmental pollution and how ours might differ from theirs in hopes that we might create a common definition.

Will: What are some of the problems facing the black community?

Prof.: We don't know all the problems, and we are not statistically sure of those we think we know: Air pollution is the highest in the black areas, because of their close location to factories and because most of the larger highways feed into the inner city, thus, the black population must pay more in terms of property value depreciation, health care, personal cleaning, and upkeep of property. . . .

Will: You said that you don't have much statistical proof.

Prof.: No, we don't. I am going to start working on that as soon as possible, but first I must get the protest movement started.

Will: I tell you what—you go and work on the egghead stuff and we will do this. OK?

James: Prof Wilson is a pretty mellow dude after all isn't he?

Will: Right on! (Hit James' hand)

* * *

Scene 3: Baby crib on stage. Various shots of different types of air pollution in the St. Louis area. (Smokestacks, car exhaust, etc.) Sound of baby coughing and breathing heavily. The coughing gets progressively worse as the slides go on.

Narrator: Would you put your baby's head in a smokestack? The people who own these do. There are more respiratory diseases in the United States today than ever before, and the major cause is air pollution. Emphysema, which used to be found only in coal miners and old men who smoked, is up about 500 percent in the last ten years. Not only does air pollution destroy your nasal hairs, inflame your sinuses, and coat your lungs with black goo, it also irritates your eyes, causing redness and wateriness. In some cases, the air pollution poisons the skin possibly causing skin cancer.
(At this point the coughing becomes spasmodic, reaches a climax, and stops abruptly)
The child is dead! . . .

* * *

Scene 4: Kitchen. Two ladies enter. One is carrying a bundle of greens.

First Lady: These sure are some fine greens I got here. (She hands the greens to the second lady)

Second Lady: Yeah, they'll make really good eating. We got some good salt pork to cook with them, sweet potatoes to bake, and I'll make some good egg cornbread later.

First Lady: You know I almost lost my whole garden this year. There were some little green bugs eating the greens up.

Second Lady: (thumbing through a paper) Well what happened? They don't look ate up to me.

First Lady: I grabbed one of those bugs up and took him to the hardware store and asked the man what he had to kill 'em. He gave me some stuff and he told me that it was the same stuff that farmers used and that it would really do the job.

Second Lady: Well if that's the same stuff you put on those greens, then it might kill us if we eat too much.

First Lady: Aw, come on. I been eating greens all my life, and ain't nothing happened yet.

Second Lady: Well, it says right here that that stuff is called pesticide, and it contains a poison called DDT. It also says that DDT builds up over periods of time and can have serious or even fatal side-effects.

First Lady: Seems like they'd be able to find something else to kill those little bugs don't it.

Second Lady: Yeah and I hope they do, child. 'Cause I sure ain't going to stop eating 'em.

Narrator: It does seem as though they can do something though, doesn't it? However, the garden sprays don't affect blacks like those pesticides that are used in most black homes. It seems like the main problem in black homes is roaches. In many homes roaches are regular occupants and control more area than the members of the family. In the summer they become especially worrisome because they bite, and the bites can and generally do become infected very easily. They are disease carriers and are some of the filthiest creatures that walk the floor. . . .

* * *

Scene 5: (Shots of solid waste in St. Louis black community) Narrator walks on the stage, sits on a bench waiting for the bus. As he waits, a number of people walk by disposing their litter on the street totally ignoring the trash can that is in easy view.

Scene 6: An alley. Trash cans are filled to the brim. Debris is scattered all over the alley. Trashman comes along emptying cans. He is very sloppy about his job and spills half of the refuse. Several kids come out and begin to play ball. A man comes out to collect his garbage cans and notices the boys in the alley.

Man: You boys shouldn't be playing ball out here. It's not a good place.

First Boy: But we don't have anywhere else to go. There ain't no playgrounds around here, and we can't play in the streets.

Second Boy: There just ain't no place to go.

(The man shakes his head regretfully and leaves the stage. The boys continue to play and as one of them is running with the ball he falls by tripping on a can and cuts himself on a piece of glass really badly. The boy hollers long and loud. The other runs to his aid . . .)

* * *

Scene 7: Living room of slum house. Six young children watching TV: Father enters the room from work.

Father: Hi kids.

(Kids say hello to their father)

Father: T.J. Where your mother?

T.J.: She had to take the baby to the hospital. She was eating paint off the wall again. She got real sick.

Father: . . . Which hospital did they go to?

T.J.: I don't know daddy.

(Phone rings. Father answers the phone)

Father: Hello. (Mother's voice on tape offstage)

Mother: Honey, the baby just died. The doctor said it was from lead poisoning. It came from eating the paint off the wall.

Father: Oh, no! You can't mean that, come on home baby. Your mother just called to say your baby sister is dead. I told that damn landlord a thousand times to fix these walls a year ago. He's been making promises to fix them—now my baby is dead from eating this plaster and paint. Now what can I do?

T.J.: Daddy, my friend, Mrs. Johnson down the street had

some problems with their landlord about their house and they went to the Gateway Center and they told them to contact the Legal Aid Society.

Father: (softer) What can they do?

T.J.: I don't know daddy but you can call them and see.

(Father gets on phone, tries to set up an appointment to see a Legal Aid lawyer)

Father: Is this the Legal Aid Society?

Narrator: How many more? How many? Oh God are all of my children gonna die in this rat-infested hole? Is this all black children have to look forward to—pollution and rats. . . .

* * *

Scene 8: Slide of baby which has been rat-bitten. Next to that a film of rats running.

Narrator: This baby will die also within the next twenty-four hours. He will die from rat-bite, the most common enemy of slum occupants.

In the ten largest cities, 5–10 per cent of children aged one to six, living in poor housing, have lead poisoning. Most children are poisoned by eating paint off walls. The paint, which has to be at least twenty years old, is found on most substandard housing throughout the country. In poor housing, one child out of thirteen will become poisoned, with the chance of permanent brain damage, or death. . . .

* * *

Scene 9: The last scene opens with Mike leaning over his mother who is being prepared to be taken to the hospital. One ambulance attendant and a hospital doctor are present. The attendant is standing back a few feet from the litter which is on the ground, a few feet to the left is a basket of freshly washed clothes. The scene is a backyard situation, in a very substandard neighborhood. Mike's sister is standing next to him.

Doctor: (Motions for the attendant to help with the litter).

(Mike reaches out and touch the doctor and ask)

Mike: Doc! (Real softly) What's wrong with her?

Doctor: It seems (in a real emphatic tone) that she's having trouble breathing.

Mike: What does that mean? (Sounding real concerned)

Doctor: It means that she has a respiratory ailment.

Mike: Is it because of the smog?

Doctor: We won't know; it could be, and won't know until we get her to the hospital and run a few tests. You know someone will have to come with us to sign her in.

Mike: My sister will go with you and I'll be over later.

(The three of them start off the set leaving Mike on the ground in the same spot and position with his head down. He stays there for a moment and then rise slowly, speaking as he rise)

Man, in all of his wisdom, can go to the moon, can transplant a heart, cure disease and make just about anything. And yet, in all this wisdom, he destroys that life he seeks to make better. (Pauses for a moment) Man, the wise one, pollutes the land, then expects it to produce. Of all the creatures on God's Earth, man is suppose to be the wisest.

But how wise is the one who pollutes his water and expects that water to clean his body? How wise is the one who contaminates the land so that it bears no fruit, and then pollutes the air and expects to breathe?

(Shaking his head in disgust)

Man with his wretched mind.

(With a loud voice)

How long must we wait before the world is free of pollution! Must we first stand on the brink of extinction, and be devoured by rats and cockroaches and wars that never end. Must we continue to be divided one from another by leaders who seek only political gain. Leaders who seek to sustain their own lives and snuff out the breath and life of the people. O God if you are truly alive, then hear the cry of the people. For our rich white brothers deny the black, the Indian, the Chicano, and the poor, food to eat. . . .

Our rich white brothers aren't concerned about poor people being unemployed, they don't care about the lousy schools. Or cops who whop the heads of the poor, and they don't care about the expressways that displaced our neighborhoods and the problems of pollution they bring in. As a matter of fact, they never cared at all about the problems until they started calling them environmental problems and saw that the mess in the food, water, and air wasn't just killing poor folk but was killing them too. They even had the nerve to think that dope would never hit their communities.

When you think about all the things happening today in this world, it kinda makes you stop and wonder. And when you do stop and think about it, you begin to understand a few things. (Pause for a moment and then with a loud cry) You began to understand why black folks and young folks are shouting "black power" and "Power to the people." You began to realize that black people and poor people are tired of living in filth, and being denied the same rights. You know, you are the ones who wrote that thing about "We the people." And black folks, poor folks, and all the young people are going to hold you to it.

(Softly) You see, we know if there isn't clean air, water, and land, then there's no clean food either. Aside from that, everything we breathe, eat, and drink is going to kill us. And if we can't get you to help us clean up this environment and give poor people their rights, then what good is law and order. (Pause) As long as people are oppressed, there can be no law and order. The law wasn't written for poor folks and black folks. If we had a peaceful demonstration today, we would be spit on, stepped on, knocked in the head, and thrown in jail. And what do the good white folks say, "They deserved it."

But if we burned down this town tonight! There would be relief programs, job training, and you name it tomorrow. Tomorrow? Tomorrow? Tomorrow? (Still repeating "Tomorrow," as he slowly walks offstage)

Narrator: What would you do if suddenly a loved one of yours became too weak to breathe our air?
(Smoke billows onstage)

MEMBERS OF ST. LOUIS METROPOLITAN BLACK SURVIVAL COMMITTEE

1. Ida Dunn
2. George Mitchom
3. Alfred Kahn
4. Arthur Grist
5. Wilbur Thomas, Jr.
6. Freddie Mae Brown
7. Angie Perry
8. Ivory Perry
9. Dr. Emil Jason
10. Booker Thomas
11. Emma Conley
12. Ted Daniels
13. Lilian Mitchell
14. Luther Smith
15. Ora Hamilton

Special credit must be given to the following persons for their hard work in putting the play together:

Al Chappelle .... Director
Helen Page .... Chief Writer
Thad Honeycutt .... Writer—Poet
Luther Smith .... Writer—Coordinator
Malicha Owens .... Writer
George Mitchom .... Writer (College Scene)
Deborah Mitchom .... Writer (College Scene)
William Jackson .... Stage Manager and Properties
Raleigh Granberry .... Photograph
Horace Browder .... Artist for Set
F. Lincoln Bailey .... Artist for Set
Odessa L. Harris .... Typist
Gloria Harner .... Typist

Special thanks for their assistance on this presentation should be given to the following groups:

Union-Sarah Economic Development Corporation and Staff
Union-Sarah Contractors Association
Black Light Culture Center
Community Affairs, Human Development Corporation
Civic Out Reach
West St. Louis Community Center
Page-Park Y.M.C.A. and Staff and Security Personnel
Regional & Urban Development Studies and Services (Southern Illinois University)
Sigma Gamma Rho of Southern Illinois University
Delta Sigma Theta of Southern Illinois University
Minority Group Planning Program of Southern Illinois University
Coalition for the Environment, St. Louis Region
Lincoln High School, East St. Louis, Ill.
Rush City Improvement Association
Center for the Biology of Natural Systems, Washington University
Union-Sarah Community Corporation and Staff

MRS. FREDDIE BROWN, a neighborhood worker at the Office of Economic Opportunity, heads Black Survival and organized the guerrilla street theater in St. Louis.

PART V

THE ENFORCERS

It is almost as if the Interior Department, Agriculture, the FTC, the FDA and the many state and local conservation bureaus were listening to Ford Motor Company president Arjay Miller, who warned in 1967 of the "threat of over-regulation by government" regarding pollution.

—Colman McCarthy
Washington Post
April 22

FRANK E. MOSS

We Don't Own the Place

University of Utah, Salt Lake City, Utah, April 22

. . . I look around in Congress to see who is now on my side. Senators and congressmen who opposed pollution control and "wasting money" on clean water and clean air now are proclaiming loudly their commitment to a clean environment. And I wonder—could we be for the same thing? The answer will come when we move from rhetoric to money, from legislation to enforcement, from convenience to sacrifice. That is when the crunch will come for us in Congress and for you in the Earth Day movement. . . .

The Water Pollution Control Act is one example of good legislation already on the books that has never been fully funded. Let me list just a few more of them for you: the Clean Air Act of 1965, the Air Quality Act of 1967, the Highway Beautification Act, the Solid Wastes Act, the Wilderness Preservation Act, the Wild Rivers Act, and the Land and Water Conservation Act.

I have long been convinced that the federal government can never be the force it should be in our environmental cleanup—can never give the country the leadership it must have—until we reorganize the federal structure which deals with natural resources and the environment so it can perform today's tasks in this field efficiently and effectively. . . .

I first proposed a Department of Natural Resources—I added the words "and Environment" to the title later—in 1965. The bill did not go anywhere that session. I reintroduced it in the next Congress, and hearings were held on it by a Senate government operations subcommittee. Only two days of hearings were held, and they were devoted to those who opposed the idea—we never got around to hearing those who favored it. But we found out in those two days that while almost everybody agreed that we lacked a coordinated, synchronized effort in the federal agencies with environmental responsibilities, each agency opposed any bill which reorganized it. In other words, the bureaucrats all indicated they would rather fight than switch.

Since then we have established a National Environmental Council, and it is just getting under way. It has been called the "keeper of our environmental conscience." But, we still need reorganization of our administrative functions—and this can only be done by bringing all of our environmental resource activities into one federal department with one head.

Organizationally, what I propose is the abolition of the Department of the Interior by transferring its agencies either to the new Department of Natural Resources and Environment or to other agencies.

Several bureaus and agencies would be transferred either into, or out of, present federal departments.

For example, the Bureau of Indian Affairs and Office of Territories now in Interior would go to Health, Education, and Welfare. The Forest Service would be transferred into the Department of Natural Resources and Environment, where it and the Park Service (which is already there) would not only work out a modus vivendi on the methods of conservation about which they now disagree, but would be parts of the same federal department with the same overall objectives.

The functions of watershed protection and flood protection now in the Department of Agriculture would also be moved into the Natural Resources Department. The civil functions of the Corps of Engineers now in the Department of the Army would likewise be moved into the new department, with the provision that in time of war or other national emergency, the functions of the army engineers would be transferred back to the secretary of the army's authority for the duration of the emergency.

It is a kind of folly that permits the Corps of Engineers to plan a $100 million flood-control project in the Rio Grande watershed of New Mexico, while upstream in the watershed there is extensive erosion which is causing sedimentation that will move downstream unchecked to fill up the reservoir, while the Soil Conservation Service of the Department of Agriculture and the Bureau of Land Management of the Department of the Interior debate their jurisdictions.

And it is certainly a kind of folly to permit the Corps of Engineers to imperil and destroy in the Florida Everglades which the National Park Service has preserved and guarded. You remember the great battle which took place on the southernmost tip of Florida. The dredges and the bulldozers and the earth-moving machines which the army engineers employed to build a canal along the northern edge of the park drained or cut off water supply to vast marshes and everglades and thus pushed back and eliminated many rare birds, fish, amphibians, and animals—some of them of dwindling species. . . .

The nonmilitary functions of the National Oceanographic Data Center now in the Department of the Navy would be transferred to the new Department of Natural Resources. The Sea Grant programs now under the National Science Foundation would be moved into the new department.

By administrative action, the water pollution functions of the Department of Health, Education, and Welfare have been transferred to what is now Interior. My bill would add air pollution functions also to the new Department of Natural Resources and Environment.

The difficulties of having administrative authority on pollution control divided among several federal departments is obvious—and the problems are multiplying. . . .

We know of examples where the army engineers, being less concerned with pollution than other matters, have failed to prevent the dumping of pollution wastes into waters under their control.

The secretary of natural resources would, under provision of my bill, be the only official whose approval would be required before the Federal Power Commission could issue a license for a project that might affect the comprehensive plan of any river basin commission developed under the Water Resources Planning Act.

At the end of each calendar year, the secretary of natural resources and environment would submit to the president and thence to the Congress a report on the year's departmental activities. . . .

These are by no means all of the organizational changes

which should be made in the federal administration of environmental, natural resources, and oceanographic programs. I have just mentioned a few of the most crucial ones.

The reason existing legislation has had so little impact is not because it was weak, but because it has been starved for funds. The reason there was no money available was because our national spending priorities were out of order. And they still are. . . .

This is not, of course, a new phenomenon. Under the Eisenhower, Kennedy, and Johnson administrations military spending took up approximately one-half of the federal budget. But it is past time for a change. And it still hasn't come.

The Nixon fiscal '71 budget recommends $73.5 billion for the military and only $1.1 billion for pollution control.

That means the president wants to spend almost seventy times as much on the military as he does on pollution.

It is when this question of spending priorities comes to the Congress that I expect Strom Thurmond and the others to leave our side. They will talk environment, but vote for more guns. They really won't have changed very much.

But you gathered here today can make them change. If you and others across this nation organize yourselves to work through the political process, you can choose representatives who will vote to change our spending priorities.

SENATOR MOSS is a Democrat from Utah.

WALTER J. HICKEL

TAPS

University of Alaska, College, Alas., April 22

. . . Alaska has long been a frontier symbol for our nation.

But this pioneer land is also becoming the state where new approaches to improving our environment are being tried—bold ideas not saddled with mistakes of the past.

We love our land, and we are concerned about the dangers of development without proper planning.

With Alaska's perspective, and with some native ingenuity, we can approach Alaska's development in a way that will demonstrate to others *that there is still a better way!*

When man appeared on Earth, he was relatively helpless, in a hostile environment.

His primary need was *security*—for himself and his family . . . and security has remained our main concern right up to 1970.

Development and the environment cannot be considered separately. . . .

For example, when we consider development and the environment in Alaska, we are considering all the ramifications of the proposed TAPS Pipeline Project.

Now, after more than a year of research, the engineering and scientific experts on our technical advisory board have established that the pipeline can be built with complete safety.

There is no longer a question of "if."

And I am announcing tonight that I will issue the permit for the pipeline right-of-way. . . .

The key, as in all efforts to meet the resources of our nation, lies in following the true definition of conservation: "Wise use, without abuse." . . .

The situation is not hopeless and don't let anyone try to convince you that it is.

In this regard, there seems to be a popular trend to condemn *all* government as a "lost cause."

But I *know* this is not true.

For example, in the Department of the Interior, we have *hundreds* of dedicated men and women who feel strongly about our environmental problems.

Government's role must be to maintain itself in constant readiness not only to *react* to problems, *but also to anticipate them before they become problems.*

If there is a pollution problem in Fairbanks, Alaska, I can't do anything about it unless I know about it.

It is appropriate, as we meet on Earth Day, to remember that man is a messy animal.

But it is also appropriate to stress that today's "far-out idea," may be tomorrow's realistic solution—*to clean up the mess.*

WALTER HICKEL is secretary of the interior.

Hickel to Permit Construction of Alaska Pipeline

Interior Secretary Walter J. Hickel has announced that he is pressing ahead with the controversial 800-mile oil pipeline across his home state of Alaska. . . .

The chief fear of the conservationists is that the original design would have placed most of the pipe, carrying oil heated to 180 degrees Fahrenheit, underground in the frozen tundra. The critics contended that this might melt the permafrost and break the 48-inch diameter tube.

However, experts from the government and the oil companies who own the line met last week at the Geological Survey's Menlo Park Research Center and satisfied themselves that the technical problems could be overcome. They talked of building 400 to 600 miles of the line on pilings above the ground, wherever there was no rock.

The conservationists also complain that the line will pass through regions subject to earthquake. But the oil and government experts say that shock absorbers can be built into the pilings on which the line will rest, making it stable.

To complaints that a pipe above the ground will interfere with caribou and other migratory animals, the government replies that either ramps can be built over low-lying portions or the animals can pass under high pilings.

The pipeline, to carry oil from Alaska's North Slope to the port of Valdez, is currently frustrated by two actions in Federal District Court here.

Sixty-six Indians from Stevens Village, Alaska, are arguing the line should not go through their land without their consent. Three conservation societies contend that the access road to be built parallel to the pipe violates a 1920 law. Both groups have won temporary orders, restraining the government from granting permits now.

Other critics of the $1 billion project charged yesterday that Hickel appeared to be revoking his own pledge to hold public hearings before moving ahead with the scheme. However, Interior officials said Hickel had promised hearings only on the specifications for an above-ground pipe and he has not yet refused to conduct them.

The line's chief owners, all with big strikes on the North Slope, are Humble Oil, a subsidiary of Standard Oil (New Jersey), British Petroleum and Atlantic Richfield.

Washington Post April 23

JOHN H. CHAFEE

NAVY VERSUS POLLUTION

University of Rhode Island, Kingston, R. I., April 22

. . . The U.S. Navy is deeply involved in the battle against pollution. We have made a good beginning and we are in for a long pull.

We began with our shore stations. When we analyzed our waste-water clean-up program—our effort to eliminate pollution from the waste discharges of our shore facilities—we estimated that 65 million gallons of waste discharged each day, about a third of the whole daily volume, would require additional treatment to meet clean-water standards. We now have the money to build proper facilities to treat 90 percent of our wastes—if all goes well within two years we'll be started on that final 10 percent.

You may have read in the newspapers recently of our success in pioneering a new antipollution process down at Norfolk. The headline read "Garbage Is Used to Do the Laundry." There we burn our garbage in a special steam plant in such a way that a minimum of air pollution is created and the amount of solid material to be dumped as sanitary land fill is greatly reduced. The plant uses 140 tons of refuse a day producing about 10 percent of the steam used on the naval base to do the laundry, keep food warm, and wash the dishes. Several cities are considering adopting the same system. . . .

As far as our ships are concerned, with a few exceptions all of our new ones, beginning with last year's building program, will have pollution abatement devices. And as our larger existing ships come in for overhauls and conversions they will be similarly equipped.

Here in the Narragansett Bay area also the navy is in the process of setting its house in order. We are working on plans for the construction—in cooperation with the Aquidneck Island Regional Disposal Authority—of a modern incinerator with air pollution control devices eliminating the need for open burning and the existing inadequate incinerator. . . .

As part of next year's military construction program we plan to institute pretreatment of the industrial wastes from the Naval Air Rework Facility at Quonset before pumping them to the air station sewage plant. So much for the navy.

JOHN CHAFEE is secretary of the navy.

MIKE GRAVEL

THE AEC: THE ULTIMATE POLLUTION

University of Wisconsin, Madison, Wis., April 21

My special interest in the field of ecology is radioactive contamination. I am deeply conscious of the fact that, along with Nevada, only Alaska has been used to test nuclear weapons, and that the possible long-term effects of those explosions are awesome.

As you know, the Atomic Energy Commission is dedicated to the promotion of nuclear energy. That is its charter under law. But it alarms me that the AEC is also the sole judge of the consequent hazards.

In reality, *no one* is in charge of preventing the radioactive contamination of our planet. In other words, the stage is presently set to *assure* the cumulative contamination of the globe. We do not even know to what extent we have already *done* it. We have done enough so that each of us carries a burden of man-made radioactivity in his body, and every baby is born with it. Every cubic meter of our air, every gallon of our river water, every meal which we eat contains it.

The ultimate complacency was expressed on January 14, 1970, by AEC Commissioner Thompson:

> In the name of protecting the environment, many are suggesting that even minimal amounts of radioactivity . . . should not be even temporarily introduced into the environment . . . It is as though we decided not to get out of bed anymore because we might slip on the way to the bathroom.

But I *do* understand that we and our government have permitted all kinds of chemical pollutants to get out of control, and that if we take the same wait-and-see attitude toward the burgeoning *nuclear* industry, no remedy will be possible.

The AEC believes that it will be able to transport and contain *most* of the radioactive poison from reactors year after year. Already we are heirs to some 80 million gallons of seething radioactive waste in tank farms. A single gallon is enough to poison a city's water supply. These tanks will have to be guarded for six hundred to one thousand years. The trouble is, radioactivity eats away just about every container that man has been able to devise. Several storage tanks have leaked thousands of gallons into the soil already.

It is scarcely reassuring that the former head of American Electric Power said recently, "We're going to have some accidents with atomic plants. We don't want to have any. But we're going to." His apprehensions were echoed just last year by David Lilienthal, the first head of the AEC, who said: "Once a bright hope shared by all mankind, including myself, the rash prolifieration of atomic power plants has become one of the ugliest clouds hanging over America."

It is strange that the Atomic Energy Commission does not even intend to investigate the possibility that radioactive fallout from the Pacific bomb tests may be causing the current starfish plague in the Pacific Ocean. . . .

Last autumn, Drs. John Gofman and Arthur Tamplin—two leading scientists inside the AEC's own biomedical research program—did some calculations which alarmed them. Their calculations concerned the increase of cancers in humans who, for one reason or another, had been exposed to radiation.

No matter how they considered the data, they came to the conclusion that the AEC's plans to promote energy under the present radiation guidelines would reverse every single advance made in public health during the last generation. In other words, they calculated that if we proceed to contaminate the environment until we each receive the *legally permissible dose* of radiation, cancer would increase by 10 percent. That means we could expect an additional 32,000 cases in the United States *every year*—plus miscarriages, stillbirths, deformities, mental retardation, and other tragic effects of radiation. Just suppose these two men are *right?*

They presented their testimony in November before the

Senate Public Works Subcommittee on Air and Water Pollution, which is considering my bill to create an independent commission to investigate certain AEC activities. At those hearings, they recommended an immediate and drastic reduction in the permissible radiation dose for the public.

How have their ideas been received?

The head of the National Council on Radiation Protection at first dismissed their thesis by claiming that he did not have time to comment; subsequently, the *full board* of the council asserted that the Gofman-Tamplin material "has presented no new data, new ideas, or new information."

The possibility of a 10 percent increase in the incidence of cancer surely seems to me something new and worth discussing.

Immediately following the Gofman-Tamplin testimony, the Atomic Energy Commission announced that the two men were wrong.

Gofman and Tamplin promptly challenged both the AEC and the Council on Radiation Protection to an open debate before scientific peers on the accuracy of their figures. There have been no takers so far. The AEC has not even made public its own set of figures on the extra incidence of cancer to be expected from the permissible radiation dose. The AEC seems worried, however. According to a nuclear trade magazine, the five AEC commissioners recently met to discuss lowering the permissible levels of reactor pollution. Two of them favored stiffer overall radiation standards, but the other three prevailed.

There is now a monumental power struggle that touches the White House, the Office of Science and Technology, the Environmental Quality Council, the National Academy of Sciences, the Atomic Energy Commission, the HEW, the Congress, the power industry, the bomb industry, the labor unions whose workers receive occupational exposures, the ecologists, the fifty sovereign states, and not least of all, you and me. . . .

SENATOR GRAVEL is a Republican from Alaska.

JOHN W. GOFMAN and ARTHUR R. TAMPLIN

The AEC: Can We Survive the Peaceful Atom?

University of Minnesota, Duluth, Minn., April 22

There is a reasonable segment of the thinking population which consider the environmental-ecologic fanfare a first-class cop-out—a convenient diversion of anger over the injustices of racism, of poverty, of an idiotic, dehumanizing war, of man's general inhumanity to other men. We have no doubt that this is a precisely correct diagnosis of the meaning of the lip-service paid to the "environmental crisis" by numerous politicians and others who indeed would like to have the heat taken off the issue of our national absence of any rational sense of priorities or values.

Today, however, we should like to point out, using atomic energy as a prime example, that the environmental crisis is not really a diversion from what might be regarded as truly important issues of our time. Rather, it is a manifestation of the ultimate retribution and irony that faces a society which, at best, can be charitably said to be free of a system of human values and, at worst, possessed of a grossly inverted set of values centering around instant greed and human power over other humans. The ironic aspect arises because no favored group will be able to find a plastic bubble in which to hide from the consequences of an unbridled Madison Avenue hucksterism bent upon the creation of products and diversion of energies into activities that are both totally unrelated to worthwhile human needs and goals.

Optimism that we can survive is hardly justified. Yet, because hope springs eternal, it seems worthwhile to describe one of the most serious manifestations of the rape of the environment by what may be called the ultimate pollution, in the faint hope that yet another illustration of human folly might somehow brake our determined, headlong race toward conversion of the Earth to the stark, lifeless beauty of the moon.

All of you know that the atomic era was ushered in during World War II with the development and use of atomic bombs. The newly-found ability to destroy life in a wholesale, efficient, inexpensive manner was indeed awesome. The Congress of the United States recognized this potential and, in what appeared a sound move, decided that the further development of atomic energy must be kept out of the hands of the military establishment. Thus the Atomic Energy Act created a civilian Atomic Energy Commission and charged it with the dual responsibility of meeting the national security needs in atomic weapons and at the same time of bringing to society all the benefits which nuclear energy must surely have in store. A last proviso was duly added that all this should be accomplished with careful attention to the safety and health of the public. No doubt the motivation of the Congress was the highest. The result, however, has been a fiasco of mammoth proportions. In retrospect one might say the outcome was predictable, but that is because of the enormous power of hindsight.

Several hopeless ingredients are now evident in the mix which has led to the present danger to life provided by the technology of atomic energy as developed under the aegis of the Atomic Energy Commission:

1. The same cast of characters held the responsibility for the military and "peaceful" aspects of the development of atomic enegry. Indeed, throughout the structure, people shuttled daily between the tasks of developing nuclear explosives for military purposes, testing such explosives, seeking out beneficial by-products of atomic technology, and protecting the health and welfare of the public.

2. The military aspects provided a wondrous cloak of cover for any stupidity, rashness, and lack of concern for human health and safety that could occur in this overall activity. Criticism of direction, of goals of errors, was easily silenced through the use of security classification and secrecy, and it is still so silenced.

3. A conflict of interest was inevitable for an agency,

in this case the Atomic Energy Commission, charged with the dual responsibility for gung-ho development of a most treacherous technology and for simultaneous protection of health and safety of the public.

4. The stage was set for the creation of a bureaucratic superagency of government, virtually free of many of the check-and-balance restraints that are requisite in a democracy.

And with the worship of the idol of growth, as exemplified in the Gross National Product, atomic energy developed the motto that "good is up," no matter how this did or did not relate to societal or human needs. As with so many other aspects of the huckster philosophy, it was believed that somehow a mad rush to "more" would certainly help us on the road to the best of all possible worlds, even a "pollution-free world."

Two major commodities were available for exploitation in the atomic energy field:

1. Energy release, either explosively, through nuclear bombs, or controlled, through nuclear reactors operating on the fission of uranium and other fissionable substances.
2. By-product radioactive substances in unbelievably copious quantities, ranging from those of extremely short lifetimes to those continuing to emit radiation for hundreds or thousands of years.

Let us focus only on the "peaceful" developments of atomic energy based upon these two commodities, energy release and by-product radioactive substances. As a minor digression, let us also recall that radioactive substances emit ionizing radiations capable of instantly or slowly destroying virtually all forms of life. And such radioactive substances can irradiate living beings externally from their presence in the environment or internally after being ingested or breathed from such sources as contaminated food, water, or air.

Since "good is up" and "more" is "the American way," the Atomic Energy Commission pressed forward on all fronts to sell its two basic commodities in the widest possible fashion, as rapidly as it could.

It has promoted the energy commodity in two forms. The nuclear reactor, releasing the energy of uranium fission, was groomed for the role of providing man and society with unlimited quantities of energy, primarily in the form of electricity. Electricity is, of course, obviously good, for who can deny the virtues of the light bulb? That the major uses of electric power are industrial, producing more pollution and garbage, is conveniently set aside in the virtuous growing—GNP philosophy.

The nuclear bomb also releases copious quantities of energy, albeit a bit rapidly. Obviously, though the atomic energy developers, such bombs have to be good for something, especially since no one was particularly enthusiastic about firing them off all over the landscape a la Hiroshima-Nagasaki. And so was born the wondrous child known as Plowshare—the "peaceful" nuclear explosive which would move mountains, divert rivers, create harbors, carve canals, loosen underground natural gas so it could become available, and do many other marvelous tasks for man.

For both forms of utilization of the energy commodity there were some nuisance-filled complications—the discriminate or idiscriminate release of radioactive substances into the environment. But, it was reasoned, the rivers, the lakes, the atmosphere, the oceans, and the Earth were all very large, and, hence, by the magic of dilution we could surely escape the consequences of pollution of the Earth with longpersisting poisonous radioactive by-products.

The by-product radioactive substances were promoted with a vigor equal to that for the energy commodity. Industry could use strong radiation sources for many tasks, and medicine surely could use radiation sources and radioactive substances for the treatment, diagnosis, and study of disease. The curve of shipment of such radioactive by-products has risen steadily over the years, to the great satisfaction of atomic energy promoters, for this meant obvious success of the endeavor. That some of the radioactive materials get lost in shipment, and irradiate unknown numbers of people in unknown places, was a minor nuisance. That the utilization of these radioactive substances meant the radiation of workers, of bystanders, and of medical subjects obviously could not be of concern, for the handling would, of course, be with great care and, in any event, it should be obvious that the benefits achieved must clearly outweigh the risks (even though neither was subjected to measurement or other scrutiny).

Oh yes, the last charge of the Congress to the Atomic Energy Commission—accomplish the objectives with careful attention to the public health and safety. The hazard came from the ability of radioactive substances and radiation to kill humans. For a promoter of technology, such a hazard is, stated simply, an unmitigated nuisance standing in the way of "progress," and is to be dealt with as such. Three ingenious methods are available for dealing with such obstacles to technological progress:

1. *Study the problem.* Surely science and technology can develop satisfactory answers for everything, including the irreversible degradation of our environment by a pollutant that can never be cleaned up, even by the most devoted antilitter campaigners.

2. *Minimize the problem.* This has several faces. First, the pronouncement is made that all aspects of life and living involve some risk—even getting out of bed. Second, we can't stand in the way of progress. Third, so there is some hazard, but surely the benefits are so wondrous as to outweigh the risk.

3. *Develop the concept of the "tolerance" dose* of a poison (radioactivity, in this case). How does this miraculous invention work? . . . The first step is to determine what dose of the poison converts humans immediately from the vertical to the horizontal position, where they remain irreversibly. This dose is designated as above "tolerance." Give yourself a little leeway by setting the "tolerance" dose, say, five times lower than this lethal dose. The technology can now go forward unimpeded until the second step is reached. At some point in the technology, more and more humans become exposed to the poison, and it becomes evident that while they are not instantly converted from living to dead, they still do die from the exposure after a period of weeks, months, or a few years. Clearly, we are then ready for the second step. This step does not require great innovation, for it is simply a repetition of the first step. One simply arrives at the remarkable conclusion that a new "tolerance" dose is required, *somewhere* below the first "tolerance" dose. The *key* requirement in this promotional approach is never to ask the question, "Is there truly *any* safe tolerance dose?"

So the new "tolerance" dose is announced with much fanfare, duly proclaiming the undying devotion of the promoter to advancement of the technology with the greatest concern for human health and life. If the new "tolerance" dose is, let us say, ten times below the previous one, two points can be guaranteed.

a. Since it took a while to demonstrate the lethal effect of the old "tolerance" dose, it will take a longer time, in all likelihood, to prove it for the new "tolerance" dose.
b. The technology can grow materially, and expose a much larger fraction of the population to the poisonous by-products for quite a period of time.

This overall cycle can be repeated as many times as are required, provided no one interferes or raises embarrassing questions. Finally, the technology is in full bloom. Its wondrous benefits are brought to every remote hamlet. The industry has grown on a steadily rising curve—the full realization of the American dream. That by now essentially the entire population has been exposed to the by-product poison, that cancer, leukemia, fetal deaths, genetic deformities and deaths have become quite prominent as a result, that the environment is irreversibly contaminated for all future generations (if indeed any can be produced)—all these can now come as a complete surprise. For surely the technology has been promoted with the greatest of care, with due consideration of health and safety of the public via the magic concept of the "safe" or "tolerance" dose of the by-product poison. Even at this point it is highly doubtful (and of course inconsequential) that the promoter will think to question the wisdom of the "tolerance" dose approach.

In the case of atomic energy development we haven't quite reached this final, irreversible disaster point, although no thanks are due the Atomic Energy Commission for this. What has happened is that during the post-World War II years, a number of elegant scientists, such as E. B. Lewis and Linus Pauling, began to question the eminent wisdom of the "tolerance" dose approach, and to point out that, in all likelihood, there exists *no* safe dose of radioactivity. Expressed very simply, they suggested that every dose of radioactivity would produce its share of leukemia, cancer, and irreversible degradation of the genetic pool of humans, with all its future untold misery and death.

Faced with the obvious danger of such a view to the future progress and growth of the technology, the atomic energy proponents had two major trump cards to play. First, one discredits the concept of no safe tolerance by impugning the motives of those who raise questions. In the cold war era of the 1950s and 1960s this approach worked miracles, for it was obvious that anyone who questioned the wisdom of the Atomic Energy Commission's activities must be a witting or unwitting dupe of the Bolshevik conspiracy. The second trump card lay in the wise development of the first approach to coping with technological obstacles to technological progress—namely, "Study the problem." The Atomic Energy Commission had carefully nurtured this approach by setting up a Division of Biology and Medicine which generously supported numerous laboratories to study the problem of hazards of radioactivity to man. The scientists, so generously supported, could be counted upon either (a) to say nothing concerning hazards, or (b) to make pious pronouncements that radioactivity was being studied and understood better than any other environmental hazard, or (c) to deny the hazard by a variety of platitudes and irrelevancies. The scientists performed these tasks well.

To say that no good biological research was accomplished by the Atomic Energy Commission scientists would be grossly false. A great deal of excellent, important work was accomplished. Indeed, from such work, it is possible to demonstrate that the whole "tolerance" approach is incorrect. But one has to extract the information from such work; it is not proclaimed either by the Atomic Energy Commission or the vast majority of the scientists it supports. The reason for the silence of the scientists is not hard to find. Negative information hurts the technology. If the technology is thwarted, the Congress cuts appropriations. If appropriations are cut, the research by the biological scientists isn't supported. This is obviously unacceptable. And, therefore, scientists are silent.

Recently we have investigated the implications of the tolerance dose concept in atomic energy development, utilizing the *current* legally established value for the population. We arrive at the following conclusions, based upon human evidence already at hand:

1. There simply is no evidence even remotely suggesting *any* safe or tolerance dose of radioactivity or radiation.

2. The current legally established "tolerance" dose, if received by everyone in the U.S.A. from any combination of sales programs of the Atomic Energy Commission, would lead to *one extra* case of cancer plus leukemia for every ten that occur spontaneously. For the population of the U.S.A. this would amount to 32,000 extra cancers and leukemias per year. Over and above these deaths, there would be additionally a large, as yet undetermined, number of genetic deaths annually plus a large number of deaths from causes other than cancer and leukemia.

3. Viewed overall, this tremendous burden of suffering and death would represent a public health setback roughly equal to the combined advances of all types in public health over the past twenty-five years.

4. All this has been made possible by the assignment to one superagency of government, the Atomic Energy Commission, of the dual role of huckstering the commodities it has to sell while at the same time doing everything possible to protect the public health and safety.

If this "tolerance" dose concept for a poison in the hands of a promoter of technology can lead to such dire results in the degradation of human health, the hereditary pool of genes, and the environment in an irreversible fashion, it would seem reasonable to suggest that Earth Day is an appropriate time to understand how this phenomenon has led to our environmental crisis and to suggest constructive preventive action for the future. And because Earth Day should be the beginning of *action* for the future of a livable world, we wish to suggest urgent action each of you can take by informing your legislators in the U.S. Congress of the following needs.

1. Outlaw the concept of a "tolerance" dose of any byproduct poison of new or existing technology. If the promoters of a technology believe a safe "tolerance" dose exists, let them prove it conclusively to lift the ban for their particular poison.

2. Abolish the dual role of promoter and protector for any agency, governmental or otherwise. Since the Atomic Energy Commission is a prime offender, it should be

stripped of all functions having anything to do with public health or safety.

3. Establish the rational principle that the only proper tolerance dose of any poison, radioactive or other, is *zero*.

4. It might be thought that establishment of a *zero* tolerance dose of a by-product's poison will mean the end of technological advancement. This is sheer nonsense, and is not being advocated. What *is* being suggested is the institution of a new principle of technological development—the principle that pollution of humans and the environment represents an issue of the highest importance to humans and is a privilege to be negotiated with the most careful deliberations. The prospective polluter should, for the first time, be asked to *prove* his case in favor of polluting, rather than the prospective human victims' being required to produce the corpses that will result from the introduction of the poison.

The prospective polluter should, therefore, be required to present concrete evidence of the *benefit* of his pollution in terms of number of lives saved or improved, and concrete evidence of the *hazard* of his pollution in terms of lives to be lost through his pollution.

If the prospective polluter can demonstrate neither the concrete benefits nor the concrete risks, he and his technology should be advised to go back to perform the necessary homework. If the evidence is presented, then the fullest possible public deliberations and hearings should be held, with all segments of the community, scientific and nonscientific, having an opportunity to consider the evidence. The public directly, or through its elected representatives, should then vote whether or not the specific pollution, at a specified level, should or should not be allowed.

Radioactivity pollution as a by-product of atomic energy development is a prime example of the erroneous approach of the past—an approach which can lead to ecological disaster. There are numerous other possible examples—indeed just about every by-product poison has been handled in a similar fashion. If an erroneous approach for radioactivity can lead to the prospect of wiping out twenty-five years of public health advances, it is not hard to see that an erroneous approach for the large combination of technological by-product poisons can do much more than wipe out public health advances. Indeed, the result can easily be wiping out the public.

JOHN GOFMAN is a physicist at Lawrence Radiation Laboratory and with the division of medical physics at the University of California, at Berkeley, Calif.
ARTHUR TAMPLIN is a biophysicist at the Lawrence Radiation Laboratory at Livermore, Calif.

PART VI

BUSINESS AS USUAL

So many mine voids underlie Scranton, Pa., a city of 103,000 in the heart of the hard-coal country, that it's thought impractical to fill them. It would be "more economical" to abandon the city, says H. Beecher Charmbury, Pennsylvania secretary of mines.

—Michael K. Drapkin
Wall Street Journal
April 22

At the Pepsi Cola Bottling Co. of Washington, marketing director James P. Anderson . . . outlined the company's current antilitter campaign.

Describing Earth Day as "something we really need," Anderson produced a copy of Pepsi's "Keep America Beautiful" public relations kit for local bottlers.

In addition to litter bags, bumper stickers and a brochure on a 28-minute beautification movie starring Lassie, the kit contains a letter to bottlers from Pepsi president James B. Sommerall.

"You can be a leader in the civic activities of your community by participating in local antilitter programs," the letter advises.

"By doing so, you will win many friends and influence those people who might otherwise attempt to push through legislation banning nonreturnables (bottles) and cans." . . .

Washington Post April 23

VANCE HARTKE

TECHNOLOGY ON THE LOOSE

Concordia Senior College, Fort Wayne, Ind., April 22

A runaway technology, whose only law is profit, has for years poisoned our air, ravaged our soil, stripped our forests bare, and corrupted our water resources. . . . Our environment will be restored only when a "cease-fire" has been called between this country's advanced technology and our environment. It is my firm belief that the chief cause of the contemporary crisis can be found in the major incompatibilities which exist between our economic system and the environmental system which supports it.

An economic system which has profit as its highest priority is ill-equipped to fight a total war against industrial pollution. By analogy a nation which reveres advances in the Gross National Product, much as primitive nations worship fertility goddesses, cannot be expected to approach the pollution problem with unbounded enthusiasm; for national growth may well slow if the pollution fight proceeds as it should.

In this country anti-pollution efforts cost money, and money cuts into profits. That is, unless the fight to control pollution becomes another lever to jack up profits and further fuel the fires of inflation.

Most reasonable men would agree, however, that the cost of pollution control technology should come from corporate profits which have been enhanced by the use of the public's environment as industry's private sewer.

It has been estimated that if the U.S. paper industry were required to meet present water pollution standards, the industry would need to spend $100 million for each of ten years. The total profit in the paper industry is $300 million per year; so that, as a minimum, the bill for antipollution devices would reduce the profits of the paper industry by one-third for ten years. Susceptible as they are to stockholder pressures it is doubtful, then, that these companies would voluntarily act to clean up their industry.

Although a strong and forceful argument can be made that it is in the long-term interests of industry to stop their polluting *now* before they completely run out of air and water and land to foul, it is questionable whether industry is willing to sacrifice short-term profits to long-term gains.

Thus, the battle lines are drawn between those who are intellectually and emotionally committed to repairing our ravished environment and those whose first and enduring allegiance is to private profit and corporate power. . . .

The politics of survival will have enemies, very powerful enemies. Not surprisingly, many of them will be familiar faces and familiar forces. For this struggle for survival will demand a degree of public spending and public management and control that will constitute a political and social revolution.

Clearly, the developing confrontation will be between those who are committed to making our presently inadequate social, economic, and political institutions equal to the task of repairing our ravaged environment, as against those whose first and enduring allegiance is to private profit and corporate power.

It is my belief that only the flat rejection of war-as-usual, profits-as-usual, comforts-as-usual, and politics-as-usual thinking will save this planet from its quickening slide into environmental disaster. . . .

Currently I am the sponsor of legislation—the "Regional Water Development Act of 1970"—which would provide for the levying of water-use charges on industries which pollute the streams and rivers of America. Under my legislation the industrial polluter would be required to pay a stated charge for each pound of industrial waste he introduced into a waterway. Although the charge per pound would vary with the type of waste—since some pollutants are more easily assimilated and dissipated in water than are others—the charge in every case would be high. So high in fact that the polluter would quickly find other ways of disposing of his waste. It is to be hoped that a polluter when faced with such a charge would try to make his operation more efficient. It has already been shown that many industrial pollutants can be recycled and transformed into salable products if only the industry involved would take the time, and do the research, to make its operation more efficient and imaginative.

SENATOR HARTKE is a Democrat from Indiana.

DAN W. LUFKIN

The Environment Business

Harvard Business School, Cambridge, Mass., April 22

Today belongs to the youth of America. Like the child in the ancient legend, they have had the courage to tell us that the emperor is naked. They have stood by the side of the road as we paraded the wonders of our civilization and they have told us we have been cheated. Instead of glittering success, they see grim failure. Instead of praise for what we have built, they blame us for what we have destroyed. Instead of seeing the magnificence of our technology, they have taken the measure of our inhumanity.

Never before has the perspective of an entire generation and all its youth been so in conflict. And in these conflicting views of our society there is a grim challenge to all of us—namely, end the conflicts or end everything. End the conflict between black and white. End the conflict between rich and poor. End the conflict between young and old, and as we are here to discuss today, end the conflict between man and his environment. . . .

Frankly, I believe that the involvement of business in the salvation of our environment will have far-reaching and perhaps even disturbing consequences. . . . Let me comment on the reactions of both sides to this situation.

I called on a number of key members of the business community. One interview sticks in my mind, a meeting with an officer of a major utilities association in New York. I asked this gentleman how his membership planned to deal with the students and others who would approach them during the teach-in. And he replied: "Oh, our members will participate—definitely—some may even give a nice lunch, a tour of the plant, and perhaps a ride in an electric car." The presence of Charles Luce on this platform testifies that not all utilities executives feel this way about Earth Day and its implications. But as I talk with you now, I find myself wondering how well those electric car operators are faring in the face of today's reality. Not very well, I imagine.

Nor do they deserve to be let off too lightly. To suppose that Earth Day is an incident best handled by the public relations department is the surest evidence of the corporate shortsightedness which has led us to a need for Earth Day in the first place. To underestimate the concern of the public, and especially of your generation, with the environmental crisis is to kindle the fires of tomorrow's disaster. Yet too many members of the business community apparently believe that this crisis can be solved by a tree-planting ceremony on the home office front lawn. In my own visits to business regarding Earth Day, over one-half the time I was ushered in to the public relations department.

On the other side of the barricades, I've heard, and no doubt you've heard, equally myopic philosophizing. "Earth Day is a cop-out, a ruse to divert attention from the war." You've heard that. And, "Earth Day is a WASP issue, a middle-class clean-up campaign that doesn't do a thing for blacks." You've heard that, too. All in all, the comments from both sides indicate to me that neither side commands a monopoly on intelligence. . . .

I want to warn you against the argument, advanced by some leading industrialists, that if we forgo short-term profit we may have no long-term future—that in the market economy, we will be eaten if we don't advance avariciously on all fours. I disagree with this thinking 100 percent, and this is not an ivory-tower planner talking. With others, I have built a business from a $100,000 equity investment to a company which last year earned $14 million before taxes. In that journey there were many days of no profit, forget short-term profit.

While we must have broad environmental legislation which prescribes uniform treatment—both carrot and stick—for industry, industry must do its part even, and most probably, at the cost of short-term profit. I do not believe that the rightful public anxiety over the environmental crisis will stand still for any other course. Nor do I believe it should.

This being the case, I suspect the crisis of the environment as it pertains to the business community is going to alter that community permanently. Let me take this thought the next step in a familiar context, that of the old argument about the social responsibility of the business organization. It was called "business responsibilities in American society" in my day here, although the subject matter was far removed from what I am advocating today. Then we all decided that, Yes, the organization does have definite social responsibilities; that in the pursuit of these, short-term profits can be held down in favor of longer-term investments in the betterment of society; and that this strategy in truth is the best possible management strategy for a business to adopt, because it constitutes insurance of a better future for all.

In my judgment, the urgent threat to survival posed by our depredations against the environment has brought the future right to our doorstep. As President Nixon has said, "It is now or never." Our whole notion of redirecting *some* of our resources into socially valuable projects but keeping *most* of our resources in making money irrespective will no longer wash. The trick will be to direct *most* of our resources to rendering society more humane and more livable *and* making money in so doing. What I am really suggesting is a reordering of business priorities, of taking the quality of life issue out of the public relations department and putting it right smack on the president's desk, as top priority. In all areas, and in all forms, quality of life must weigh equally with Adam Smith's market mechanism in the allocation of resources.

Does this mean the death of the profit system and of free enterprise capitalism? In a thousand speeches before a thousand Rotary clubs, it perhaps will. But in this speech, it doesn't. I do think that the mishandling of the issue by some businessmen will compound the woes of transition. But I also think we're deaded for a type of redefinition, not an abolition, of the concept of profit—one that will assess corporate gains and losses not only in terms of dollars but also in terms of social benefits realized or not realized.

At this point, I can almost read the minds of some of you who are thinking: Well and good. But how do you convert social benefit gains into measurable indicators? How do you quantify benevolence?

The assumption that you can measure business performance only by money standards—and its counterpart that you can't assess social beneficence in money terms—is like the assumption that the bumblebee can't fly. No matter what the aerodynamic engineers prove on the drawing board, it damn well does fly. And the quantification of social gains, despite the abstract logic of some theoreticians, is proceeding apace. As evidence, let me refer you to an article by Robert Beyer in the March 1969 *Journal of Accountancy*. Mr. Beyer is managing partner of Touche, Ross, Bailey & Smart in New York. Needless to add, his other management credentials are impeccable. In his article, "The Modern Management Approach to a Program of Social Improvement," Mr. Beyer explains what's being done today in Detroit to quantify the results of the city's welfare programs. Among many other insightful comments, the article includes this one:

> The degree to which basic human needs are reduced, and the time it takes for reduction to occur, is the acid test of a social program's success. Continuing measurement, reliably controlled in the best accounting tradition, provides a valuable instrument of continuing evaluation. The absence of this ingredient is responsible for the failure of more social improvement programs in the past than any other single factor.

It can be done, and I interpret Mr. Beyer's remark as a direct rebuke to the doubters. Broadly, he's suggesting that if we apply the same skill and control to managing social improvement that we're applying to managing businesses, we will be able to measure quantitatively the effect of our involvement.

There are those in business today, in the ranks of top management, who object to business involvement in not-for-money-profit social endeavors, or profit endeavors with a socially responsible overtone. They feel sincerely that such endeavors are primarily the concern of government. I disagree. It seems to me that future historians will see much of the American twentieth century in terms of brilliant theoretical proposals on the part of government, but of correspondingly dismal administrative realities. I hold with Peter Drucker that the job of government is to propose directions for society and to legislate the rewards and penalties into being. But it's the role of enterprise to act, to manage, to innovate, and to bring about social change. This, after all, is what businessmen are good at doing. As a matter of past historical fact, one of the reasons the big government we've got arose in the first place was because private enterprise—lacking the motivation of survival—shirked for so long its environmental and social responsibilities.

Now, we have no choice but to assume these responsibilities and we do have the primal motivation of survival. Far from wishing the government to do an incompetent job with them, I'm willing to hope that we recapture from government all kinds of business-related endeavors and make money in so doing. In sum, not only do I hope as a businessman for the lion's share of the work to be done on our environment, but I favor also the "reprivatization"—another phase of Drucker's—of the postal services, the lending agencies, and the other unwieldy factories of government administration.

What will business life be like after the millennium of a new definition of profit? Will businessmen be forced to say, like the old wizard in the *Lord of the Rings,* "The Third Age of the world is ended, and the new age is begun; and though much has been saved, much must now pass away"? I don't think we're quite ready to put aside our energy and initiative or to say good-bye to the American dream. But I do think that our business life, which has changed so much over the past decade, will change even more over the next. I think in many respects it will be even more satisfying to be in business than it has been. Echoing the comments of another sage, John Maynard Keynes, "I look forward, therefore, in days not so very remote, to the greatest change which has ever occurred in the material environment of life for human beings in the aggregate. . . . The critical difference will be realized when prosperity has become so general that the nature of one's duty to one's neighbor is changed."

I think the nature of our duty has changed indeed. With Keynes—Keynes the man—I feel that "it will remain reasonable to be economically purposive for others after it has ceased to be reasonable for oneself." This, I think, is to become the major motif of business. It must, if we, our system, and our way of life are to survive.

DAN LUFKIN is chairman of the board of Donaldson, Lufkin and Jerrette, Inc.

KENNETH BOULDING

WHAT IS THE GNP WORTH?

University of Pennsylvania, Philadelphia, Pa.
April 20

. . . We are interested in 1971 being in some sense better than 1970, and so we're looking for indices. The difficulty is that all indices and all measurements of which ways are up are deceptive, including the Gross National Product. I have formed a one-man society for renaming the GNP the Gross National Cost, which I think is much more descriptive of what it actually is. However, it shouldn't be despised as a measure—we shouldn't despise any measures. But we shouldn't believe any of them either.

It is extremely important to develop social indices. A total index is something that either gets larger or smaller when things get better. If it gets larger you go after it; if it gets smaller you go away from it. . . .

Even though the GNP is a very imperfect index, almost anything is better than nothing. If you contrast, for instance, the thirties with the sixties, you will see that at least the GNP is helping to prevent the sort of mistakes that Mr. Hoover made. Herbert Hoover didn't know which way was up. In his memoirs he actually says that in 1932 apple selling became very profitable and a lot of people went into it. . . .

We now know that from 1929 to 1932 something went down—we're quite sure of what. The GNP is useful for the crude purpose of saying what goes up and what goes down, but it certainly needs to be replaced by a more accurate index which will take care of the bads as well as the goods.

The GNP is moderately good indexing goods, but it also includes a lot of bads like the war industry and pollution.

When we pollute something somebody else has to clean it up. That increases the GNP. . . . Obviously a lot of these bads ought to be netted out. . . . The critical question is, What do you net out of the GNP to get the figure that is most significant for human welfare. . . . I'm a little pessimistic about getting any immediate, perfect measure of which way is up, but I am interested in identifying the processes in the social system which produce the downs.

Even if we can't get a single measure, can we identify the deteriorating processes in social systems? Can we build up defenses against them? This is the critical question of social inventions. In the next hundred years we will very much need social inventions for the discouragement of bads and the encouragement of goods of all kinds. . . .

KENNETH BOULDING is a professor of economics at the University of Colorado.

BARBARA REID

Roots of Crisis

Outside the General Electric Stockholders' Meeting
Minneapolis, Minn., April 22

What we see here today is the beginning of a movement, it is a movement determined to make the corporate, governmental, and educational institutions of this country responsive to the needs of the people. To get at the roots of the environmental crisis we face on this planet, we must begin to talk about the decision-making structure of our society. Pollution and the Vietnam war are symptoms of misplaced priorities and a warped conception of human values. To many of us it seems that individuals have lost control over their lives, that they are manipulated by a system with an inherent death wish rather than one in which enhancement of life is the primary goal. The major symbol of this death culture is the institutionalized violence perpetrated upon people and the land by corporations such as General Electric.

Corporations can no longer operate in isolation; corporations can no longer reject the demands of the people. . . . General Electric stands high on the list of those institutions that have propagated our overconsumptive and "planned obsolescence" culture. It is the fourth largest corporation in the country. It is the second largest defense contractor in the country. It is directly tied to the military-industrial complex, employing ninety former high-ranking military officers. Two of its directors formerly held the office of secretary of defense. Its military business has grown by leaps and bounds since the beginning of the Vietnam war. From 1962 to 1968 they netted over $8.5 billion from military business. It foists upon the consumer mounds of technological gadgets which supposedly contribute to the "good life."

We can no longer afford such waste. We can no longer afford such toys. One of GE's major products, the light bulb, does not last even half as long as those produced in Europe. This is planned obsolescence. We must be prepared to make GE contribute to a more ecologically sound world. We must begin to make some sacrifices ourselves, and those adjustments in our life-style cannot continue to be judged in terms of profit alone. GE must also begin to make some sacrifices. We must begin to judge our actions and the actions of corporations like GE in terms of their effect on people's lives.

We stand here today to let GE know that the people are aware of the mindless consumption of gadgets that it helps to foster. We stand here today to let GE know that such practices will be tolerated no longer. We stand here today to symbolize the death of those ecologically unsound practices and affirm life: for us, and for our children.

BARBARA REID is midwestern coordinator for Environmental Action.

RON M. LINTON

Paying the Price

Hunter College, New York City, April 23

. . . Since the Industrial Revolution, we have allowed commerce the free use of the physical environment—discharging effluents at will. Even today, we are accepting the view that "progress," defined as increased industrialization, is sacrosanct—an immune part of the great American economic dream. If there's money to be made, damn the environment. Dollar and profit are supreme. Just as we exploit people in this country, so we exploit the land. And just as we must enact laws to protect individual freedom, so must we enact laws to save our natural resources. . . .

It is imperative that we devise a system where production of goods and services meets our physical needs, but at the same time permits us to enjoy a physical environment which makes material things worthwhile. The environment should be a place where men can live in dignity and harmony, where the great achievements of modern civilization and the ageless pleasures afforded by natural beauty are available to all. . . .

But already we can hear his voice saying: "It costs too much;" or saying: "It is the public who will pay."

But we are paying now. Yet there are those who continue using your environment, and mine, for nothing.

Certainly the price of goods and services is going to go up if we are to improve the environment. Nothing can be done for nothing. But let us beware of those who use the improvement of the quality of life to mask unnecessary price increases. Let business be warned that we will not tolerate using environmental costs as an excuse to cover other sins or balloon profits. . . .

Occupational illness illustrates the interrelatedness of all environmental hazards. The worker is the first to be exposed to man-made indignities which later pose a threat to the entire population. There is growing evidence to indicate that occupation may directly contribute to the incidence of various chronic or deteriorating diseases previously believed to be entirely connected with work exposure. Yet today, fewer than 15 million of the 53 million wage and salary workers in industry are provided with sufficient in-plant health services. And virtually none of our agricultural workers have any protection.

George Bernard Shaw once said, "Science is always wrong. It never solves a problem without causing ten more." Such is the case with the new contaminants flooding the market, like microwave ovens, color televisions, and lasers. Our technology has outstripped our ability to deal with it. Can we be sure that the nuclear reactors being built or planned throughout the country will not have deleterious effects? No: yet they will be built. We must take the stand that unless the manufacturers can prove their products are safe, they cannot market them. The people of this country can no longer remain quiet in the name of "progress." We must not tolerate industrialists who exploit the land and its inhabitants, make profits, and then make *you* pay for their mistakes. . . .

Years ago, big business geared itself for a supersonic transport airplane. We, who should have been aware of the gruesome health implications, allowed research to progress to the point where the president and industry could convince most people to stop research would be a waste, and that to continue would be costly but beneficial. We will soon be blessed with daily sonic booms because we didn't predict and mobilize soon enough. And we will probably solve this problem in the same fashion that we have solved other problems—by selling 250 million earplugs.

RON LINTON is president of Linton, Mields and Coston, Inc., environmental consultants.

ADAM WALINSKY

THE BLUE-COLLAR MOVEMENT

State University of New York, Buffalo, N.Y.
April 22

. . . The environment movement is in serious danger of ignoring the most serious threats to the environment of the United States today. At the outset, of course, it passes by the fact that the most serious threat to the moral, psychic, political, and physical environment of the United States today is the continuing war in Vietnam. It passes by the constant environmental threat of total nuclear destruction, and of the continuing escalation of the threat—with MIRVs and ABMs and all the obscene acronyms of modern war. Equally important, the movement is well on its way toward passing by the two groups which, even in the narrowest terms, face the worst environmental problems in the nation today.

One of these groups is the poor. Black children in Harlem eat lead paint as it flakes off tenement walls. Puerto Rican children in the same city live with the deepening plague of narcotics addiction. Farm workers are exposed to pesticides that are the commercial counterpart of nerve gas. These people, and millions like them, are trapped in their environment more surely than we are locked upon this earth. . . .

The second group with a truly serious environmental problem is the men and women who work in plants and factories, in the heart and bowels of the American industrial system. There are, in the United States, over 30 million industrial workers; there are over one million in New York State alone. . . .

The problem is for the moment beyond statistics, because the statistics are not even kept. No one yet knows now many coal miners have died or been crippled by black lung. No one knows how many steelworkers have been crippled by silicosis, how many chemical workers have died of emphysema, how much of the enormous rise in cancer and stroke and heart failure is in fact the result of what men breathe while they work. We do know, however, the reason why there are no statistics. It is that there has been a silent conspiracy of ignorance—a conspiracy of inaction and lassitude and unconcern—that has kept the facts from our sight. . . .

- In West Virginia, the coal industry tried to deny for years that there was a connection between coal and dying of black lung. It took a union insurgency to make the Mine Workers' Union support a bill that would offer its own members some minimal Workmen's Compensation for their disease and death. It took a major wildcat strike to make the West Virginia politicians pass the compensation bill. And the man who led the union insurgency is dead of assassins' bullets.
- The federal government, under the Walsh-Healy Act, is supposed to protect the safety of 30 million workers whose plants receive federal contracts. There are sixty inspectors—one for every half a million workers covered—and no major facility has ever been shut down nor any major contract canceled for failure to maintain a decent plant environment.
- Here in New York State, concern with worker protection from pollution is a bad joke. The state employs 118 men, most without adequate education, training, or expertise, to inspect over 200,000 factories and workplaces in the state. The average factory is inspected once every two years, without any equipment more sensitive than the inspector's nose, for an average of 105 minutes, including paperwork. Some of the most dangerous and polluted areas within plants have not been inspected for periods of seven years. Air samples are almost never taken. The state sets pollution standards for only 400 of the 12,000 major industrial chemicals and substances now in use; often the standards are almost meaningless. The United States Navy will not permit healthy young men to be exposed to carbon monoxide in concentrations of more than 25 parts per million; the

state of New York says that workers of all ages, many not in the best of health, may be exposed to twice that level.

- Meanwhile, industry and employers often seem less concerned with the health of their workers than with an unremitting search for profits. Recently, public statements were made about the pollution in a specific plant —the Union Carbide plant in Buffalo. A report of the Committee for Efficiency in Government (of which I am chairman) pointed out that of eighteen men working in a unit of that plant, seven have already contracted emphysema; one has died, perhaps from cancer; and ten more have acute bronchitis—an early state of emphysema. The response of management was to threaten local union officials with a lawsuit for defamation. There has been no serious industry response to the poisoning of construction workers by asbestos—though its hazards are so well known that Great Britain has banned its use for over a generation. There has been no response to the carbon monoxide poisoning of bridge and tunnel workers and garage attendants. There has been no serious recognition of the simple human tragedies of men who begin to cough their lungs out at the age of thirty, whose skin is already pitted with the advanced dermatitis that is a step away from cancer, whose families are left fatherless and without support when the men die at forty or fifty. . . .

All this is of consequence to more than the men and families involved. Rather it goes to the heart of the nation's politics in the year 1970, and to all the rest of this decade. The central problem of liberal politics today is how to rebuild a coalition of decency. . . .

Middle-class white college students, or well-to-do reform politicians, are in a poor position to lecture the average steel or auto worker on the needs of justice in the United States. We do not share his troubled neighborhoods nor his difficult and dangerous job; our education has allowed us to escape the burdens of inflation and much of the draft alike. Always, over the past decade, it has been he and not we ourselves who has been asked to pay the real price of awakening racial justice. If we now allow the environment movement to become—as it is in real danger of becoming—a pretty plaything of the affluent, if we now ignore the real environmental problems of the ghetto and the farm laborer, and the blue-collar worker in his factory, then we will have thrown away one of the best chances for political change in this decade before its starts; we will be choosing political suicide, and the name of our sword will be irrelevance.

ADAM WALINSKY, Democratic candidate for attorney general of New York, was an adviser to the late Robert F. Kennedy, and was New York coordinator for the Vietnam Moratorium Committee.

CHARLES A. HAYES

A Time to Live

Civic Center Plaza, Chicago, Ill., April 22

Working people, black people, and poor people have known about pollution long before it became so fashionable to talk about it.

The steelworkers have been living under the belching smokestacks of the steel mills for the past fifty years or more.

The packinghouse workers have been breathing in the stench of rendering plants both at home and at work since the turn of the century.

The workers in the grain mills have been developing lung ailments for many decades from the fine dust in the air, both inside and outside the plant walls.

What we are belatedly discovering today is that the winds from south Chicago don't stop polluting when they reach the Loop or even the North Shore. What we are discovering is that when enough of these poisons are thrown into the air by the steel mills, the power plants, and the oil refineries, it is not just the workers in the plants, or the poor living in the shadow of the plants, who must breathe these poisons, it is all of us!

The story is the same for the blood and offal thrown into the rivers of the Midwest by the packing plants, the polluted dredgings of the Army Corps of Engineers, and the toxic wastes of the steel mills and other industries, not to mention the ships continually dumping their raw sewage into the Great Lakes. The drinking water and the swimming facilities of the workers living near plants may be affected first, but the currents reach eventually the private beaches of the most exclusive yacht clubs.

A better environment for all of us will not come easy.

What we have to recognize is that there are deeply rooted economic interests who will oppose us tooth and nail, but whose public relations departments will continue to issue fine statments about how dedicated they are to the search for a better environment.

Nor will a better environment come from community antilitter drives, desirable as these may be.

The environment in which hundreds of thousands of families exist in inner cities across the country *includes* the rats which attack their children, the lead in the peeling paints which poison their babies, the decrepit housing conditions, the inadequate nutrition, and the lack of green space.

We are told by Senator McGovern's study of the hunger problem that 15 million people in America cannot afford an inadequate daily diet. It is small comfort to breathe clean air while you slowly starve to death.

The black people and the poor of this country can understand and join in the fight for a better environment, so long as that fight recognizes the need for joint action on all the basic evils of our environment.

Cleaning up these evironmental evils will require money—vast sums of money—far beyond any routine program for improvement of waste disposal and sewer systems. We are told by the scientists that we are faced by an environmental crisis—that the limited volume of air surrounding our earth, the limited amount of water available to sustain life, and the limited expanse of land available to produce food are all threatened. We are told mankind itself faces extinction if we continue our present practices.

Our nation has been spending $30 billion a year to inflict death and defoliation on a small Asian nation. At the same time our national administration's major new contribution to the preservation of life on this continent is the offer of $4 billion, spread over five years, for a better sewer system.

I don't want to use polite and fine-sounding words like we must have a "reordering of our priorities." If we believe what the scientists are telling us—and I think we had better believe it—the time for polite and empty talk is past.

The scientists tell us we must choose between life and death. I'm not about to sweet-talk when somebody has his fingers around my throat. I say "STOP THE KILLING

RIGHT NOW AND LET'S START SAVING LIVES RIGHT NOW!"

The war in Vietnam must be ended immediately, not just phased out over the next five or ten years. The president still talks about bringing home *all* the *combat* troops *eventually*. Does he think we will forget about the quarter million *support* troops that he omits mentioning and that he seems inclined to leave over there forever? He talks about bringing home 150,000 combat troops in the next year, maybe, maybe, if, if, but gives no figure of how many will come home next week, or even next month.

Couldn't we better use the energies and skills of all of the 400,000 men still in Vietnam right here at home, and right now, in building better homes, improved mass transportation facilities, more schools, more antipollution equipment, and helping to meet all the other needs of the life-and-death crisis we face in our environment?

The additional billions we continue to pour into military hardware, the billions our government wants to put in ABMs, MIRVs, and SSTs, must be used instead to protect and reclaim not only the air we breathe and the water we drink, but the human beings who can drink that water and breathe that air. How do we protect and reclaim children and youth, old people, sick people, the unemployed and the underemployed? Our program to protect and reclaim the physical environment must include feeding the hungry, healing the sick, building homes and schools, eradicating racism and discrimination, and finally making the national welfare program adequate to lift people forever out of the degradation of poverty.

These are some of the tough decisions that will have to be made. If we include these goals in our program of demands and stand firm in our determination to achieve these demands, the demagogues, and those who simply join the antipollution bandwagon to make political hay will soon fall by the wayside.

This is what the fight to preserve our environment really means—it is a fight to preserve and protect humanity. And all of us, black and white, rich and poor, young and old, must enlist in that fight NOW! WE SHALL OVERCOME!

CHARLES HAYES is vice-president of the Amalgamated Meatcutters and Butcher Workmen of North America.

PART VII

AUTODAFÉ

We do our best to stay one full step ahead of the legal requirement.

—JACK QUICK
Assistant Comptroller
of General Motors

CHARLES H. PERCY

AND DON'T BREATHE THE AIR

University of Illinois, Chicago Circle Campus
Chicago, Ill., April 22

. . . Air pollution is one of the forms of pollution that most concerns us. In the large cities of this nation, estimates as to the amount of air pollution caused by car engines run as high as 80 percent. Obviously, if we could eliminate automobile discharges as a form of air pollution, a giant step would be taken toward achieving clean, pure, fresh air.

The auto industry has for years been devoting time and money to research and development of a cleaner internal-combustion engine and to alternative power sources such as the external-combustion engine.

As a matter of fact, the automobile industry currently spends about $150 million annually for research and technology in controlling emission pollution, or about $15 per car per year. . . . In the area of style and design changes, the auto industry annually spends more than $1 billion annually, which amounts to about $140 per car per year.

In the past, the money that the auto industry spent to investigate how to clean up the air might have been sufficient.

Now, however, we acknowledge that pollution must be stopped and stopped now. With this as a basic supposition, we can then look at priorities. Which is more important, a new car with attractive style changes, or a new nonpolluting engine? In answering this question we must consider the moral implications of our answers.

If the automobile industry were to switch over to a radical new power system such as [the steam engine], it is estimated that the cost would be in the neighborhood of $2 billion. This seems a great deal of money, but we should keep in mind that the money spent in one year on style changes is more than a billion dollars a year.

Considering the immense problem we are faced with, we have to come up with some new, bold, different ideas. Perhaps one such idea would be for the automobile industry to consider spending as much money on the development and eventual changeover to a system such as the external-combustion engine as they now spend on style changes. This of course would mean very little money available for style changes. Perhaps it might even mean that the auto industry would join together and declare a moratorium for several years on all nonessential style changes, and pledge that the money normally used for these purposes be spent on urgent research and development programs. Then we might be a great deal closer to the goal of clean air for our lungs.

Such a step would be radical and unprecedented. It would mean that additional billions would be available for the immense task with which we are faced. It would mean that little or no federal tax money would be needed.

But if the consumer is not willing to sacrifice such luxuries as style changes in cars so that he can breathe clean air, then we are just paying lip service to the problem of pollution. . . .

The problem is great and immediate and unprecedented. It is immoral to allow this problem to continue. We must, then, take the great, immediate, and unprecedented steps that the morality of survival demands.

We must each, as individuals, as communities, as corporations, as a nation, make those painful decisions that are required. . . .

SENATOR PERCY is a Republican from Illinois.

DONALD A. JENSEN

Ideas from Ford

University of Southern California
Los Angeles, Calif., April 22

Ladies and gentlemen, let me state at the outset that Ford Motor Company shares your concern over air pollution. We recognize that we have an obligation to help *solve* the problem and will continue to go all out in attacking the problem—from every practical standpoint — until it *is* solved. This is a commitment of the chairman of our board, Mr. Ford, and is a firm commitment of our entire organization. . . .

Dozens of research projects are underway, many conducted by California firms and California laboratories as well as by auto and oil companies and the federal government. One $13 million air pollution research program, encompassing some thirty projects, is being directed by the Coordinating Research Council and is being financed by the Automobile Manufacturers Association, the American Petroleum Institute, and the federal government on a selected project basis. . . .

Donald Jensen is on the air pollution control board of the Ford Motor Company.

WALTER P. REUTHER

Two-ton Gadgets

United Auto Workers Convention, Atlantic City, N.J.
April 20

We must recognize that in our kind of society, in the complex technological world in which we are fighting for the very survival of our environment, we cannot rely upon the selfish, socially irresponsible blind forces of the marketplace. . . .

The auto industry is one of the worst culprits and it has failed to meet its public responsibility. . . .

Perhaps most important of all, the auto industry with its enormous technological capability ought to join with the government and it ought to join with other industries in developing a modern mass transportation system all over America. It is asinine (I don't know of a better word to describe it) to have hundreds of thousands of people all going to the same place at the same time for the same purpose and all of them dragging two tons of gadgets with them. . . .

The late WALTER REUTHER was President of the International Union of United Auto Workers.

The following collective bargaining resolution was passed by the UAW convention on April 28, 1970:

> Our members should be aware that in response to the pollution caused by the internal combustion engine, states are now beginning to pass legislation which would prohibit the manufacture of the automobile as we know it today. Unchecked pollution by the automobile and related industries is of direct concern to auto workers not only because they are citizens concerned for their environment but because there is a direct threat to their jobs and their job security.
>
> **In the light of this, we shall insist that the problem of pollution will be a matter for collective bargaining in 1970 negotiations. The workers' stake in resolving this problem for society and the nation is compounded by the stake in his own job. We shall raise this issue sharply in 1970 negotiations in discussions with the companies.**

PAUL P. CRAIG

GET THE LEAD OUT

State University of New York, Stony Brook, N.Y.
April 22

In the last few months, we have heard a great hue and cry raised against leaded gasoline. Even Detroit opposes lead. Most of the opposition, although well motivated, is based upon erroneous reasoning. Lead is an industrial mystery story, with the outcome as yet not fully known. Lead was introduced into gasoline in 1924, strictly for economic reasons. It remains today for this same reason, and because lead makes it easier for Detroit to fuel its insolent high-compression chariots. In the process, it has very probably produced substantial damage to people, especially to chlidren.

At high levels of exposure, lead poisoning's effects are well known. Historically, it has been blamed for the fall of the Roman Empire. The Roman women in the first century B.C. developed a taste for wine. Roman wine was stored in leaden vessels. The dissolved lead entered the wine, and rendered the women infertile. To make matters even worse for themselves, the Romans also used lead as a sweetening agent, and as a cure for diarrhea. The Roman upper classes died out within a couple of centuries. Lead consumed by Romans represents one of the earliest known cases of massive self inflicted poisoning.

Today, acute lead poisoning is found mostly in ghetto children, who eat paint from the walls of tenements and develop a host of symptoms, of which the worst is brain damage and loss of intelligence. Unless therapy is begun quickly, the damage is permanent. In some cases death occurs.

Lead plays no known biological role. It is a rarity among

the trace metals in that it serves no known useful physiological purpose. Any presence of lead in the body can be considered a source of potential danger. Today the average American carries about in his body (mostly concentrated in his bones) about 200 milligrams of lead. This amounts to about three parts per million by weight. This burden is remarkably close to the toxic level. If your body burden of lead were tripled to about nine parts per million, you would die of classical lead poisoning. Since most of us carry in the vicinity of nine parts per million of DDT in our bodies, it is apparent that lead is substantially more toxic than DDT.

This small margin of safety might be of little concern if this was the way nature designed us and our biosphere. Unfortunately, there is compelling geochemical evidence showing that virtually all of this burden we carry is the result of the activities of man. Geochemists have estimated that in a natural environment lead burdens were a factor of one hundred below what they are today. Some evidence supporting this thesis is found from studies of lead in the bones of prehistoric man. Such studies are difficult, for man has a long history of eating from lead-glazed dishes, using solder and pewter, and doing many other things which tend to introduce lead into his body.

With lead as with DDT it is virtually impossible to find a place in the world which man has not contaminated. Lead has been found in places as remote as the Greenland ice sheet (where its abundance is about four times that of DDT). By taking borings, the lead in the ice may be measured as a function of the age of the ice. The lead level remained roughly constant until about fifty years ago, when it started to rise rapidly. Tetraethyl lead was introduced into gasoline in 1923. Man has also contaminated the oceans of the world with lead. Geochemical evidence shows that most of the lead in the upper layers of the world's oceans is there as a result of man's activities, being brought to the sea by rivers and by rainfall.

The manner in which lead gets into the biosphere is only partially understood. In the United States, we utilize about one million tons of lead in a year. About a quarter of this goes into gasoline in the form of tetraethyl lead, and the remainder is used for a wide variety of functions, including solder, batteries, and pewter vessels. Lead used as solder for metal cans can be dissolved by the food therein, rendering the food potentially dangerous. If one's diet consisted exclusively of certain canned foods and soft drinks, one would soon die of lead poisoning. Atmospheric lead, which arises almost entirely from gasoline additives, accounts for at least one-third of the lead in urban-dwelling Americans. The contribution is largest in people working in atmospheres loaded with gasoline fumes, such as garage mechanics and traffic police. Lead contamination is highest in congested urban areas and near highways. Street sweepings in cities contain a high proportion of lead, which comes from automobile exhaust and serves as an additional source of contamination.

If the lead levels in man have been raised so much by man's activities, then why, you may ask, aren't we all sick from lead poisoning? We may be. Lead poisoning is particularly insidious and hard to diagnose, except when massive doses are involved. The response of the body to lower doses is complex and poorly understood. For many years it was held by industrial toxicologists that a sharp threshold exists for damage due to lead. Today it is known that damage can occur at much lower levels than the toxicologists had believed. Evidence is accumulating from animal experiments that very low amounts of lead can produce damage, especially in animals deficient in calcium or chromium. Recently, evidence has been obtained in Finland of biochemical alterations in humans at blood lead levels found in urban-dwelling Americans.

There is developing an increasingly convincing body of scientific knowledge indicating that lead at existing levels may be producing damage, and that this damage is most likely to occur in children, or in particularly susceptible individuals. The group in our population most subject to injury from chronic exposure to lead is probably ghetto children, who are already under stress for many reasons, and who can ill afford this additional physiological burden. Lead from gasoline poses an additional gratuitous burden upon these children.

Lead is a totally unnecessary pollutant in our urban atmosphere. It represents an assault upon our physiological integrity over which we have no control. The amount of damage being done to us is unknown, but could be quite significant and still remain undetected simply because the proper scientific investigations have yet to be made. There is no question but that if lead were not now in gasoline, and a manufacturer were to propose putting it there, he would not be permitted to do so. Lead is in our gasoline for historical reasons relating to horsepower and profit. It is time to get it out.

The story of lead in the biosphere, and of lead in gasoline, is far from finished. In fact, it is only now starting to unfold. As it unfolds, it is becoming increasingly apparent that we have in lead another instance of our inflicting injury upon the most susceptible members of our society. We do this without malice, but because we have failed to take into account the complex interwoven nature of the biosphere.

PAUL CRAIG, chairman of the Environmental Defense Fund's committee on lead, is a physicist at Brookhaven National Laboratory, and an associate professor at the State University of New York, Stoney Brook, N. Y.

JESSE UNRUH

The Highway Lobby

University of Southern California
Los Angeles, Calif., April 22

As things stand now, most government institutions most of the time are unable to cope with real threats to environmental quality; in many cases they are unwilling to deal with these problems; and far too often, government itself is the cause of the problem.

Governor Reagan devoted one-third of his state of the state message this year to environmental quality. But less than one three-thousandth of the governor's budget is new state money for environmental protection. . . .

The governor's budget this year proposes the expenditure of $793 million on highway and freeway construction. In contrast, it allocates only $237,000 for rapid transit. That works out to about $3,000 spent on freeways for each dollar spent for rapid transit.

There is probably no better example of state government's *complicity* in the destruction of the environment than this continued insistence on the freeway-only solution to complex transportation problems. The policy is perpetuated by a powerful Division of Highways which employs about 17,000 people and runs on an annual budget well in excess of three-quarters of a billion dollars. The division is protected by a freeway establishment made up of business interests—oil, auto, trucking, and construction—which have much at stake in maintaining the system.

The establishment is sustained by a constitutionally protected state gasoline tax and a similar tax by the federal government, both of which are used solely to build and maintain highways. Each new freeway generates more traffic which, in turn, demands more freeways which generate more vehicle miles and more gas-tax revenues to provide yet more freeways.

Since the cost of the freeway-only solution is paid for by gas taxes, while the cost of rapid transit must be supported by local taxes, the freeway solution prevails. About 60 percent of all the land in fully developed urban areas is handed over, lock, stock, and barrel, to the automobile, a fact with great economic implications; freeways don't pay taxes.

The result is that our cities are overrun by acres of concrete and choked by traffic and life-destroying smog. The freeway is a major contributor to the deterioration of our central cities, and that deterioration will surely get worse under the present administration.

Ronald Reagan has stated as his policy that rapid transit be used only to provide transportation to those who do not now have it—the poor, presumably, who don't own cars. He has assured his friends in the automobile industry and the oil industry that their private preserve in state government is safe as long as he is governor; that he will make no effort to reduce California's destructive dependence upon the automobile.

JESSE UNRUH is speaker of the California House of Representatives.

Part VIII

LAWNORDER

All power pollutes.

—Garrett de Bell

RODERICK A. CAMERON

DEMONSTRATE

State University of New York, Stony Brook, N.Y.
April 22

Environmental degradation is the way of our time. It need not be so. The solutions for most man-made problems are already known to modern science. The difficult part is to implement them. To do so requires fundamental changes in public policy as it relates to a host of environmental issues. If our social institutions are not to be abandoned, they must be altered or otherwise made effective to cope with the environmental crises we face.

Past practices have been dictated by short-term economic considerations. It is cheaper to dump wastes into the river, release fumes into the air, or saw the tallest virgin timber. Environmental degradation is a by-product of some of our largest private and public enterprises. Entire industries and whole economic subsystems depend, in the arbitrary lexicon of the balance sheet, on the freedom to release pollutants or to destroy natural resources. Yet the savings or profits are short term, and accrue to a relative handful of people. The true social cost is far different. The price is an increasingly degraded environment for ourselves and our progeny.

What can citizens do to cope with the crisis? The obstacles to effective citizen action in the consumer area are essentially the same in environmental politics. There is a peculiar paralysis in our political branches of government, which are primarily reponsible for legislating and executing the policies environmentalists are urging. The phenomenon is simple and well known. Industries who profit by rape of our environment see to it that legislators friendly to their interests are elected, and that bureaucrats of similar attitude are appointed. . . .

Our government seems extraordinarily vulnerable to the accrual of political power by representatives of narrow but powerful economic interests. Indeed we seem to be more a democracy of economic interests than of private citizens. Accordingly, the response of our political branches of government to citizens' increasing cry for environmental sanity is inadequate. The problem is clear: How do we get our government to respond to a clear need which its most influential political inputs oppose?

Another part of the explanation is less sinister but no less serious. Decisions affecting environmental quality frequently involve technically difficult and scientifically sophisticated considerations. It pays the interested industries to take the time and provide the expertise, legal skill, and healthy budget needed to articulate their wants to the decision-making body. But too often the public concern, the ecologcal consideratons, the broader public interests go unheard. No means has yet been found to present consistently a vigorous and scientifically sound exposition of the total environmental cost of every proposed course of action before our policy-making bodies. With such lopsided representation it is understandable that even nonpolitical decision-making bodies like the courts and regulatory agencies decide issues unsoundly. Worse, for want of being petitioned about environmental problems in an adversary context, many regulatory agencies are not even aware of the environmental issues they ought to be deciding.

One of the Environmental Defense Fund's current suits is to stop the U.S. Army Corps of Engineers from constructing a barge canal over much of the course of the Oklawaha River in Florida. In writing about this corps project in his January 1970 *Reader's Digest* article "Rape on the Oklawaha," James Nathan Miller admirably stated the problem:

> Thus the tragic irony: while there is probably no issue on which the American people are more united than the need to preserve their environment, there is no fight they are losing faster. The reason: distribution of forces. On one side are the huge numbers of conservationists, split up into localized fractionalized units, working in their spare time, with their own money, mainly in their own communities. On the other side are the developers—well

> paid businessmen and bureaucrats, tightly organized in trade associations and lobby groups whose influence extends statewide or even nationwide. In the Oklawaha battle, for instance, while there wasn't a single conservationist lobbyist in the state capital at Tallahassee, there were at least 50 lobbyists for pro-canal interests. It's a case of a horde of unarmed amateurs fighting a few professionals who are equipped with the latest weapons.

The judicial branch of government, when legislative and administrative remedies fail, does offer a fair and impartial forum in which environmental wrongs may be righted. Courts are largely free of the economic and political pressures of vested interests. I believe that the judiciary is the one social institution already structured to provide the wise responses that may enable us to avert ecological disaster. Where scientific validity is an issue the rules of evidence and the rights of cross-examination can be crucial in separating fact from fiction. Where specialized agencies may tend to be myopically mission-oriented, courts stand on a higher plane. Court response to the problems of society is often powerful therapy for the unresponsiveness of the political branches of government. The civil rights decisions of the fifties and sixties sensitized society to conditions it had ignored and spawned extensive legislation to alleviate those conditions. Important social legislation has often been preceded by lawsuits which pose, structure, and focus the problem.

Some have said that to close the courthouse door to environmental issues is to open the door to the street. I believe the door to the street is already open and should be used fully as much as the door to the courts. It takes social dynamite to break the granite attitudes of industrial polluters, and indeed of ordinary citizens wed to environmentally destructive modes of behavior—like the habit of wrapping a two- or three-ton compartment of steel about oneself and with the help of a 400-cubic-inch internal-combustion engine driving two or three miles down a three- or four-lane freeway cut through the heart of a city to park on a large asphalt parking lot that was once a park. Demonstrations, big disruptive ones, are powerful forces of change. Sure, other citizens are irked at the demonstrators. But the message, nevertheless, is forcefully put. I believe there is probably a relationship between the degree of irritation shown by a citizen toward a demonstration and the extent to which the demonstration's message is troubling him. Indeed some sort of new Parkinson's law operates here. The more despised a demonstration is the more forcefully its message is attacking the prejudices of the despiser. Few demonstrations have caused more derogatory comment than those surrounding the Democratic convention in Chicago. Yet never before have Democrats been so serious about making political conventions meaningful.

Demonstrations work. Unpopular demonstrations work better. Untoward happenings at a demonstration do not, in my view, detract from its effectiveness.

So I believe the most fruitful avenues for citizen action are to open the doors to the courthouse to litigate and to the street to demonstrate.

Let me say a few words on the consumer interest versus the environmental interest. The problem of the consumer and environmentalist in bringing about change is similar, and the economic interest each must confront are often similar.

But the interest of a consumer as a consumer often conflicts with his interest as an inhabitant of his environment. . . .

Consumers like electrical appliances. Yet increased electrical generating demands foretell more pollution from the generating plants.

Consumers like low taxes. Yet it will cost many billions to save our environment.

Consumers like effective detergents. The environmentalist likes biodegradable detergents of low phosphate content.

Consumers like items conveniently and cheaply packaged. The environmentalist insists on packages which do not degrade the environment.

Consumers like single-dwelling homes. They like to consume space. Yet our environment is running out of open space and multiple cluster dwellings may alleviate the consumption of space.

The consumer consumes. Indeed our entire Judeo-Christian culture consumes. The environment does not belong to us alone and should not be consumed.

Often industrial polluters use our consumer propensity

to shop for the lowest price as justification for not spending money to minimize their pollution. They argue that if they thus increased their costs and sales prices, we consumers would pass by their products in favor of their irresponsible competitors. That argument has merit no matter how often used as a phony excuse to cover up inefficiency and irresponsibility. In that respect, we are locked into a vicious circle. The first corporation in an industry to break ranks and clean up its pollution endangers its profits through the attendant increased costs. The fault lies in one sense with us consumers. We exert marketplace pressure to force prices down. That is good for the economy generally. As a consumer I only wish our buying patterns exerted greater pressure to lower prices and were less vulnerable to big Madison Avenue marketing budgets. Expensive advertising campaigns too often nullify consumer pressure to lower prices by brainwashing consumers into paying higher prices for inferior articles. But as an environmentally concerned citizen, I must consider the effects of my buying patterns. . . .

We consumers thus must bear some responsibility for industrial pollution. One way to lessen our blameworthiness is to crank one more factor into our buying decisions: environmental impact. If there is reason to believe lead pollution is serious, let us pay the additional penny or two per gallon to buy lead-free gasoline. Let us make manifest our willingness to pay more for goods and services that do not unduly degrade our environment.

Another way to lessen our encouragement of industrial polluters is to insist on uniform, nationwide pollution regulation. In that way an entire industry can be compelled to clean its stacks and treat its sewage, and our consumer instinct to buy the cheapest item will be less suspect environmentally. The conflict between consumer and environmentalist is real. We must be cognizant of that conflict and pay the price to reduce it.

One last thought. People concerned with consumer problems tend to be liberal. This is probably because the solution of many consumer problems revolves around attack upon the caveat emptor principle which is a frequent part of conservative values. Conservationists, however, are as likely to be conservative as liberal. Despite my remarks about using street demonstrations, I do not believe that the liberal environmentalist should go out of his way to insult the conservative conservationist. As a coalition they can cause change. Indeed it will be charming to see little old ladies demonstrating against the history of the last fifty years, standing tennis shoe to tennis shoe with longhaired youths demonstrating against our vaunted technology run amok.

Edward P. Morgan said the other day that if the meek ever end up with an Earth to inherit they will have the militant to thank for it. Being militant about environmental degradation is not indicative of one's politics. It is mere good sense.

RODERICK CAMERON is executive director of the Environmental Defense Fund.

VICTOR J. YANNACONE

SUE THE BASTARDS

Michigan State University, East Lansing, Mich.
April 22

During the spring of 1968, the alumni of Yale Law School, who claim among their numbers half of the justices of the United States Supreme Court, 10 percent of the nation's law teachers, and any number of distinguished attorneys, held a reunion. The intellectual theme for that reunion weekend was "Law and the Urban Crisis."

Five prominent legal educators, deans at their respective law schools and distinguished urban legal scholars in their own right, were invited to address the alumni on this urgent question, but just as the proceedings were to begin, a group of black law students, together with members of New Haven's Black Coalition, entered the auditorium and began to address themselves to the all-white speakers platform and the all-white alumni audience:

"You just don't understand the problem at all," they said. "The problem is not 'Law AND the Urban Crisis;' law IS the urban crisis!"

And now when we look to the law for answers to many of our social and environmental problems, we do find that the law itself is the cause of many of those problems.

It is "the law" which zones the housing patterns which led to building too many highways for too many autos.

It is "the law" which expropriates public property for private profit.

It is "the law" which permits environmental degradation.

It is "the law" which asserts equal protection of that law for the corporate person—that fictional, bastard child of the law, endowed by the Supreme Court after the Civil War with all the God-given rights of a human being, but without soul to save or tail to kick.

It is "the law" which assures equal protection for the corporate person but denies it to the poor, the black, the Indian, the inarticulate, the politically weak or ineffective, women.

It is "the law" that forbids the public distribution of birth-control information in many states.

It is "the law" that denies women the freedom to determine the use to which their wombs will be put.

It is "the law" which created and maintains a tax system that encourages overpopulation and penalizes those who remain single or with few children.

Always it is "the law."

Most of our environmental problems stem from the misguided attempts of ecological Neanderthals to control the uncontrollable. Pesticide abuse is a classic example. Throughout the history of modern agricultural methods, agribusiness has ignored the potential value of integrated control techniques where specific chemical *bullets* are used to augment the armory of natural and biological insect controls. The indiscriminate use of broad-spectrum, long-presistent pesticides such as DDT, dieldrin, endrin, aldrin, toxaphene, and heptachlor have so altered the ecology of agricultural ecosystems that more resistant pest species have evolved and new species have become pests.

Utilizing our water resources for waste disposal is still another example. Oceans, and rivers, lakes, and streams, are just like any other sink—they have a finite capacity for waste, after which they back up. Moreover, they fight back as algae blooms quickly decay into sulfurous miasmas. Our atmosphere is not a limitless sink into which we can pour countless tons of noxious gases and poisonous particulates. The atmosphere too has a finite capacity for waste, and we are reaching that limit today.

Our high-speed air transportation system has begun to alter our weather patterns and climatological cycles. High-altitude clouds from commercial jet contrails have begun to reduce the amount of incident solar radiation received by green plants on the ground.

It ought to be obvious that man's apparent dominion over the environment is but a license from nature with the fee yet to be paid. We should have learned from the disastrous effect of radionuclide fallout that what we sow we must also reap, yet the fallout of lead and other heavy metals, chlorinated hydrocarbons and other toxicants continues at an increasing rate. Mankind has ears, yet does not hear the warnings shouted from the environment all around him. More and more noise is tolerated, increasing the toxic environmental stresses already imposed on urban and ghetto dwellers throughout the nation. We now even have a new unit for the measure of noise, the Perceived Noise decibel—PNdb, and the noise standard makers have now decided that the noise level of a four-engine jet transport at takeoff, as heard from 1,500 feet away, is tolerable, and of course, any noise of less intensity is even more tolerable. We are proceeding to develop a supersonic commercial jet transport, even though it has already been demonstrated that continued random awakenings can produce transient psychoses.

There is a legend found in the folk history of most cultures about the young man who made a pact with death where death agreed to give three warnings before the end.

After many years, as the man lay dying, he demanded that death honor the bargain and give warning. Death told the man that the bargain had been kept, but that the man had ignored the warnings hidden in the miraculous recovery, the narrow escape, and the inexorable passage of time.

Mankind has been warned, and mankind has been given a rare choice among all those animals headed for extinction as a result of mankind's attempt to act as lord and master of the environment, rather than conservatively manage its limited natural resources. We can either drown in our own sewage, die buried under our own garbage, choke to death on unbreathable air, or be driven to homicide and suicide by the noise around us.

There are four conventional appeals to law for protection of environment: The first, and deceptively the simplest approach, is through the legislatures of the several states and the Congress of the United States. If this approach is successful, there will be, of course, no need for other than occasional interpretive litigation. The ways of the legislature, however, are slow and ponderous, and many of our national natural resource treasures are in immediate danger of serious, permanent and irreparable damage.

The Florissant fossil beds represent a classic example of legislative ineffectiveness in a crisis situation. At stake were the unique and irreplaceable Florissant fossil beds, a 6000,-acre area thirty-five miles west of Colorado Springs, where seeds, leaves, insects, and plants from the Oligocene period 34 million years ago are remarkably preserved in paper-thin layers of shale. These fossils, studied by scientists from all over the world, are the richest of their kind anywhere on earth. A hundred and forty-four different plant species and more than 60,000 insect fossil specimens have already been found. The Florissant fossils are considered by many scientists to hold the key to determining the ultimate effects of air pollution on climate, since the air pollution from the volcanic activity that preserved the Florissant specimens was associated with a sharply cooling climate in Colorado.

Following a subcommittee hearing at Colorado Springs on May 29, 1969, the United States Senate unanimously passed a bill establishing the Florissant Fossil Beds National Monument. But while the Congress was deliberating, four land speculators purchased over half the land to be included within the national monument and announced that they intended to begin bulldozer excavation of roads to open the land for development immediately, unless the land was purchased by government or private groups.

The Defenders of Florissant, an ad hoc organization of scientists and citizens dedicated to protection of the fossil beds, finally turned to the courts, filing suit

> On behalf of all the people of this generation and those generations yet unborn who might be entitled to the full benefit, use and enjoyment of that unique national natural resource treasure, the Florissant fossil beds,

demanding a temporary restraining order prohibiting disturbance of the fossil shales by the speculators until such time as Congress had completed its deliberations.

On July 9, 1969, the United States District Court for Colorado held that no federal court could interfere with the absolute right of private property ownership and the only way to save the fossil beds would be to buy them, at whatever price the speculators demanded.

The Defenders of Florissant appealed to the United States Court of Appeals for the Tenth Circuit that same afternoon, but the court questioned its own power to grant a temporary restraining order and demanded to know what law the speculators had violated. We had to concede that Congress in its infinite wisdom had never seen fit to pass a law protecting fossils, so the Court of Appeals then demanded to know what right they had to interfere with an individual's use of his own land so long as the use didn't violate any statute law.

All that was left to do was to point to a fossil palm leaf that had been discovered at Florissant and plead:

> The Florissant fossil beds are to geology, paleontology, paleobotany, palynology, and evolution what the Rosetta stone was to Egyptology. To sacrifice this 34-million-year-old geologic record, a record you might say written by the mighty hand of God, for thirty-year mortgages and the basements for the A frame ghettos of the seventies is like wrapping fish with the Dead Sea Scrolls.

In a precedent setting ruling, the Court of Appeals restrained the speculators from disturbing the fossil beds, but the temporary restraining order terminated on July 29, 1969, and on that day the District Court heard testimony and argument for a preliminary injunction.

Meanwhile, Congress had cleared the bill through a subcommittee of the Committee of Interior and Insular Affairs and now the bill was pending before the entire committee prior to release to the House floor for action. Nevertheless the District Court again held that there is nothing in the Constitution to prevent a landowner from making whatever use of his property he chooses, and if the fossils were to be saved they had to be purchased at the speculators' price.

Again it was necessary to appeal to the Tenth Circuit Court of Appeals, and at the hearing the speculators contended that they only intended to scrape off the top layer of the fossil shales and that would still leave more than sixteen feet of fossils remaining. We told the court, "You could just as well say scraping the paint off the Mona Lisa would cause no real damage because the canvas was left." And again the 34-million-year-old fossils were rescued by a last-minute court order. A preliminary injunction was granted by the Court of Appeals just as the bulldozers were poised at the boundary of the national monument.

Although Congress finally passed the bill, the difficulty

with the legislative approach to environmental protection is best summed up in the words of the clerk of the Court of Appeals: "Will you please get that bill through Congress soon and give us some rest."

Many legislatures, recognizing the delay inherent in the legislative process, attempted to meet the needs of modern technological society by creating administrative agencies, to which they ceded some of the powers of the legislative, executive, and judicial branches of government in order to give speedy effect to the will of the people as manifest by act of Congress.

Unfortunately, the administrative approach carried within itself the seeds of its own abuse. Any administrative agency, no matter how well intentioned, is not a court, it is a star chamber—judge, jury, and executioner. All in the public interest, of course. The narrow jurisdiction and mission-oriented viewpoint of administrative agencies, particularly those charged with industry regulation, make them inherently incapable of considering environmental matters with the requisite degree of ecological sophistication.

The *Scenic Hudson Preservation* case [354 F.2d 608 (2 Cir., 1965)] marked the fork in the road for those concerned with the protection of our environment and the legal defense of the biosphere. The Second Circuit Court of Appeals held that the Federal Power Commission should hear evidence on natural values in addition to the economics of electric power generation and distribution.

The tragedy of the *Scenic Hudson Preservation* case occurred when the Scenic Hudson Preservation Committee yielded to the Federal Power Commission jurisdiction of the natural resource aspects of the Consolidated Edison application, cloaking the FPC with a mantle of ecological competence it does not possess and cannot attain within the limits of its statutory mission. The old-guard, reactionary, established preservationist-conservationists, in their all-consuming desire to avoid challenging established bureaucracy, yielded to the Federal Power Commission the ultimate power to make ecological judgments binding on generations yet unborn. . . .

If we have to find a common denominator for the serious environmental crises facing all technologically developed countries regardless of their nominal form of government, it would have to be entrenched bureaucracies which are essentially immune from criticism or public action.

These self-perpetuating, self-sufficient, self-serving bureaus are power sources unto themselves, effectively insulated from the people and responsible to no one but themselves. . . .

We must carefully examine the real sources of political and administrative authority before we can evaluate the extent to which the real government of the people approaches the totalitarian.

In this country, we need look no further than the Division of Pesticide Registration of the United States Department of Agriculture. The means of investigation was environmental litigation—not the conventional "Wall Street lawyer" approach of the Scenic Hudson Preservation Committee, but the no-holds-barred frontal assault of Equity.

In 1966, a citizen sought equitable relief from a toxic insult to the community ecosystem and sued not just a local mosquito commission using DDT, but DDT itself (*Yannacone* v. *Dennison, et al.*, 55 Misc.2d 468, 285 Supp. 2d 53).

Finally, in a New York court of equity, the full weight of scientific evidence against DDT was presented to the social conscience of the community in a forum protected from the political, economic, and bureaucratic pressures that for twenty years had successfully suppressed the evidence of DDT's worldwide damage to the environment. At long last the agrichemical-political complex was forced to put its propaganda to the test in the crucible of cross-examination.

Three years later, at Madison, Wisconsin, in another courtroom challenge of DDT, Dr. Harry W. Hays, director of the Division of Pesticides Registration of the United States of Agriculture, testified: "If the data appear to us . . . to be adequate . . . the product is registered. We look at the data furnished by the manufacturer . . . but we don't look at it analytically . . . We don't check it by the laboratory method."

At long last the people were told that the Department of Agriculture relies entirely upon data furnished by the pesticide manufacturers and does not do any independent tests of its own. The incredible lack of concern for the safety of the American people became apparent on further cross-examination when Dr. Hays admitted that if a pesticide was checked at all, it was checked by an entomologist only for its effectiveness against the target insect and not for its effect on beneficial insects or fish and wildlife. "We don't assume that the intended use will cause any damage," he explained.

Moreover, Dr. Hays further admitted that although he had personal knowledge of published scientific studies showing damage to fish and wildlife from DDT, the Division of Pesticide Registration is not doing anything about possible environmental hazards from the pesticide.

Dr. Hays had proudly testified previously, on behalf of the Industry Task Force for DDT of the National Agricultural Chemicals Association, that the United States Department of Agriculture is solely responsible for the registration of pesticides and for determining whether they may be shipped in interstate commerce. He also testified that these determinations are not subject to review except on appeal by the pesticide manufacturers, and then Dr. Hays reluctantly admitted that the public had no access to USDA records of pesticide registration.

Only in an adversary judicial proceeding was it finally demonstrated that the United States Department of Agriculture is really serving the agrichemical industry and not the American people, while remaining at the same time essentially immune from responsibility to the American people.

Conventional tort litigation suits for money damages on behalf of private citizens represent another avenue of appeal to the law on behalf of the environment, yet this avenue also leads inevitably to questions without answers.

What do you do about a toxicant like DDE—that metabolite of DDT—which is ubiquitously distributed throughout the lipid tissues of every living element of the biosphere? What do you do about a toxicant whose toxic effects cannot be demonstrated as the proximate cause of any particular personal injury or disease?

In the struggle to protect natural resources against the depredations of such shortsighted, limited-vision, governmental agencies as the Corps of Engineers and the Department of Agriculture, any attack upon agency decisions must *not* be based on damage to a particular private economic interest.

The Everglades cannot be saved from the army engineers by showing the potential loss of income to hot-dog vendors in the Everglades National Park as the National Audubon Society attempted to do in the *C–111* case. Nor could the Florissant fossils have been saved by any unscientific appeal to aesthetic sensibilities.

The futility of the attempt to protect the environment by alleging private damage is best described in the history of the rape of Pennsylvania by the coal industry during the nineteenth century. Again the story was told not in the school, or in the press, but in the dry words of the courts:

> . . . in Pennsylvania, one operating a coal mine . . . may . . . drain or pump the water that percolates into his mine into a stream . . . although the quantity of water may thereby be increased and its quality so affected as to render it totally unfit for domestic purposes by the lower riparian owners. *(Pennsylvania Coal Company* v. *Sanderson,* 113 Penn. St. 126)
>
> That case had a varied history and it was not until it came before the court for the fourth time that, influenced by the necessities of a great industry, the rule was laid down as indicated.
>
> The case was first considered in 1878, when the claim of the lower riparian owner was sustained upon the principle of sic utere tuo, ut alienum non laedus.

(So use your own property as not to injure that of another.)

In reply to the argument of counsel that the law must be adjusted to our great industrial interests, the court said:

> In reply to the argument of counsel that the law must be adjusted to our great industrial interests, the court said: In the argument here the ground was distinctly taken that immense public and private interests demand that the right which the defendants exercised in ejecting the water from their mine should have recognition and be established. It was said that in more than a thousand collieries in the anthracite regions of the state the mining of coal can only be carried on by pumping out the percolating water which accumulates in every tunnel, slope and shaft,

> and which, when brought to the surface, must find its way by a natural flow to some surface stream. It was urged that the law should be adjusted to the exigencies of the great industrial interests of the Commonwealth and that the production of an indispensable mineral reaching to the annual extent of twenty millions of tons, should not be crippled and endangered by adopting a rule that would make colliers answerable in damages for corrupting a stream into which mine water would naturally run. * * * The consequences that would flow from the adoption of the doctrine contended for could be readily foretold. Relaxation of legal liabilities and remission of legal duties to meet the current needs of great business organizations, in one direction would logically be followed by the same relaxation and remission, on the same grounds, in all other directions. One invasion of individual rights would follow another, and it might be only a question of time, when, under the operations of even a single colliery, a whole countryside would be populated.

In 1880, the case was reviewed a second time and it was again urged that the rights of the riparian owners should yield to the immense public interest involved. The court, however, reaffirmed its former decision and, among other things, said:

> The mining interests of the defendant do not involve the public interest, but are conducted solely for the purposes of private gain. Incidentally, all lawful industries result in the general good; they are, however, not the less instituted and conducted for private gain, and are used and enjoyed as private rights over which the public has no control. It follows that none of them, however important, can justly claim the right to take and use the property of the citizen without compensation. *(Pennsylvania Coal Co.* v. *Sanderson,* 94 Penn. St. 302)

In 1883, the court heard the case for the third time with the same result, but on the last review in 1886, by a vote of 4 to 3, it reversed its previous decisions and held:

> . . . the use and enjoyment of a stream by the lower riparian owners, who purchased their land, built their houses and laid out their grounds before the opening of

> the coal mine, the acidulated waters from which rendered the stream entirely useless for domestic purposes, must *ex necessitate* give way to the interests of the community in order to permit the development of the natural resources of the country and to make possible the prosecution of the lawful business of mining coal.

The extensive coal mines of the state of Pennsylvania were regarded as of sufficient importance to warrant the court in departing from the law as previously laid down by itself in the same case, as well as from the rule which prevails in England and in this country, except in some states where mining is extensively carried on. . . .

Now in spite of the lessons of more than fifty years of nuisance law development, timid lawyers and timid conservationists are still hoping that

> through conventional damage suits, such as those downstream property owners might bring against upstream polluters, what amounts to a citizen's right to a clean environment may be established.

The Court of Appeals in the state of New York has put that idea to rest recently by affirming the decision of a lower court in an action against a cement plant and quarry near Albany, the New York State capitol.

> . . . The relief sought in these actions was an injunction restraining defendant from emitting dust and other raw materials and conducting excessive blasting operations in such a manner as to create a nuisance and the recovery of damages sustained as a result of the nuisance so created.
>
> Despite its conclusion that the defendant in the operation of its plant had, in fact, created a nuisance with respect to plaintiffs' properties, the trial court refused to issue an injunction. In reaching its decision on the propriety of granting the injunctive relief sought, the court carefully considered, weighed and evaluated the respective equities, relative hardship and interests of the parties to this dispute and the public at large. Re-examining the record, we note the zoning of the area, the large number of persons employed by the defendant, its extensive business operations and substantial investment in plant and equipment, its use of the most modern and efficient de-

vices to prevent offensive emissions and discharges, and its payment of substantial sums of real property and school taxes. After giving due consideration to all of these relevant factors, the trial court struck the balance in defendant's favor and we find no reason to disturb that determination.

The trial court did award damages based upon the loss of usable value sustained.

The damages awarded now amount to a license fee to the cement company to continue its pollution. This is the same effect that the proposed $10,000-per-day fine to be levied on polluters of Lake Michigan would have. For the sum of 3.65 million dollars per year, an industry with gross sales in excess of $2 *billion* would have a license to pollute Lake Michigan, which already hangs like a festering appendix on the great bowel of Midwest civilization. The time has come to forgo such puerile attempts to torture empty legal formalism into environmental protection.

Just so that we understand each other from this point on, I must tell you that I believe the lawyer is an advocate. Some lawyers advocate in the courtroom. Some lawyers advocate in the classroom. Some lawyers advocate in the halls of government. Some lawyers advocate in the smoke-filled rooms behind the halls of government.

But when a lawyer tells you that he is above or beyond advocacy; or that he is only interested in seeing to it that the formalities of legal precedent are observed, flee from him! Law is the framework of civilization and litigation is the civilized answer to trial by combat. The courtroom is the arena. Lawyers are your champions. The rules of evidence are the articles of war.

Litigation is not a game and the courtroom is no longer the playground of dandy gentlemen. Lawyers are not disinterested observers exercising their wit and erudition before a disinterested judge, for in every lawsuit someone must win and someone must lose. Although on any given set of facts the winner and loser might be different at different times in history or in the context of different civilizations, nevertheless, rest assured, a winner and a loser there will be.

Great industries will never lack for advocates!

Government will never lack for advocates!

Political organizations will never lack for advocates, and the established institutions of the political-industrial-military-power-structure, in their rape of our human and natural resources and their prostitution of the legal profession, need no more advocates.

PEOPLE need advocates!

PEOPLE need champions!

But now a warning to all of you who would go forth as champions of the people in defense of the environment. Defending the environment is like defending an indigent. If you are a wealthy, well-established practitioner with a large law firm to support your efforts, and if the case is of sufficient community or national significance, then the defense of an indigent can be euphemistically described as a privilege reserved only for members of the legal profession.

If on the other hand, however, you lack these emoluments, the defense of the indigent becomes an obligation at best, and more often than not an onerous duty, and since the environment belongs to all of us, it appears that no individual is willing to pay for its protection or defense.

Throughout the country, you hear the people who ought to know better pleading for the attorney general or some other governmental official to clean up the country. Yes, indeed it would be a boon to all the people if each and every state and federal official was willing and able to take action to protect our national natural resources, but even the best efforts of well-meaning government officials have been thwarted to date, and there is no evidence that new laws will improve the situation.

Just what is a natural resource? Is it something that can be taken from the earth, then wasted, squandered, or used as the source of private fortune, or is it something that belongs to each of us as trustees for future generations, to be used wisely by whomever might hold nominal title at any particular time? How do you balance the need for advancement of aviation, represented by the development of supersonic commercial transports, against the needs of the general population for privacy and freedom from the shock effects of sonic boom?

What do you do when a municipality decides that the highest and best use of a mighty river is an open sewer?

What do you do when the Army Corps of Engineers or the Bureau of Reclamation decides to drown the Grand Canyon or most of central Alaska, or insists upon destroying the delicate ecological balance of an entire state like Florida?

Just what can you do?

SUE THE BASTARDS!

We must knock on the door of courthouses throughout this nation and seek equitable protection for our environment. We must not wait for Congress or state legislatures or local government to pass laws, we must assert the centuries-old fundamental doctrine of equitable jurisprudence—a doctrine as old as civilization, a doctrine as old as the Talmud, or the New Testament, or the Roman law, or the Middle Ages—a doctrine as new as today and as advanced as tomorrow: Let each person—human person or corporate person—so use his own property as not to injure that of another, particularly so as not to injure that which is the common property of all mankind—the air and the water.

At this time, the environmental interests of civilization can only be protected by direct legal attack upon those actions which can cause serious, permanent, and irreparable damage to our natural resources. Only by asserting the fundamental constitutional right of all the people to the cleanest environment modern technology can provide, and asserting this right on behalf of all the people in courts of equity throughout the nation, can we defend the environment.

The time has come to housebreak industry. The time has come to establish, once and for all time, as a fundamental principle of American justice, that industry owes the American people the cleanest air and the cleanest water that the existing state of the art in pollution control can secure. . . .

Today a great many young people feel alienated and unable to communicate their feelings, concerns and suggestions to industry and government. Students, there are two ways to tell your story to the people:

You can lie on your back in a pool of blood in the gutter holding a picket sign up for thirty seconds of late-night TV news, or you can sit on a witness chair in a courtroom and tell it like it is. . . .

Industry and government can ignore your protests, ignore your picket signs, and certainly they can repress your demonstrations. But no one in industry or government ignores that scrap of legal cap that begins:

YOU ARE HEREBY SUMMONED TO ANSWER THE ALLEGATIONS OF THE COMPLAINT ANNEXED HERETO WITHIN TWENTY DAYS OR JUDGMENT WILL BE TAKEN AGAINST YOU FOR THE RELIEF DEMANDED.

No one in industry or government ignores a summons and complaint.

Rest assured that the corporation president reads it. The chairman of the board reads it. Their lawyers read it, and their lawyers' lawyers read it. And they *must* answer it. Not in the press, where all their flackmen can distort the issues. Not in the marketplace, where all their financial might can overrule the facts. Not in any place where their lawyers or flackmen or marketing experts or anyone else can really help them, but in a courtroom where, as far as the facts are concerned, you the individual are the equal of any man or any corporation.

A court once asked me for the legal precedent on which I based my argument that industry owes us the cleanest effluent that the existing state of the art in pollution control applicable to that industry could provide. I told the court that I asserted this right as one of the fundamental unenumerated rights guaranteed by the Ninth Amendment to the Constitution of the United States, which says:

> The enumeration in the Constitution of certain rights, shall not be construed to deny or disparage others retained by the people.

and protected under the due process clause of the Fifth Amendment to the Constitution of the United States:

> . . . nor shall any person . . . be deprived of life, liberty or property, without due process of the law . . .

and under the due process and equal protection clauses of the Fourteenth Amendment of the Constitution of the United States,

> No State shall make or enforce any law which shall abridge the privileges of immunities of citizens of the United States; nor shall any State deprive any person of life, liberty or property, without due process of law; nor deny to any person within its jurisdiction the equal protection of the laws.

I reminded the court that among these unenumerated rights were the right to life, liberty, and the pursuit of happiness asserted as among the inalienable rights of man endowed by the Creator, and then I asked the court to take judicial notice that the rights set forth as inalienable in the Declaration of Independence were those won on that plain in Runnymede during the thirteenth century, and finally I appealed to the court to take judicial notice that the rights and obligations set forth in Magna Charta are simply a medieval restatement of the fundamental rights and obligations of all mankind given on that mount in Sinai at the dawn of history, the Ten Commandments. That was all the precedent the court needed to let us proceed with the case.

The men who cared so much for the future, who were so concerned about the establishment of rights against infringement by government or individual, these visionary men *forgot* to establish your right to breathe clean air or drink potable water.

For more than 180 years, each of the citizens of the United States has been breathing without a permit. Each of the more than 200 million citizens of this country today is breathing without a constitutional provision establishing that right.

All right, all of you who believe now that we need a constitutional amendment to establish our right to breathe, stop breathing! . . .

Experience has shown that litigation is the only nonviolent, civilized way to secure immediate consideration of basic questions of human rights. Litigation seems to be the only rational way to focus the attention of our legislators on the basic problems of human existence. The only way, that is, short of bloody revolution.

This land does not belong to General Motors, Ford, or Chrysler; this land does not belong to Consolidated Edison, Commonwealth Edison, or any other private investor-owned utility company; this land does not belong to Penn-Central, B & O, C & O, Union Pacific, Southern Pacific, or any other railroad; this land does not belong to American Airlines, United Airlines, TWA, or any other common carrier; this land does not belong to Minnesota Mining & Manufacturing Company, Minneapolis Honeywell, IBM, Xerox, Eastman Kodak, Polaroid, or any other company marketing technological marvels; this land does not belong to International Paper Company, Scott Paper, Boise Cascade, Weyerhauser, Crown Zellerbach, or any other paper products company; this land does not belong to United States Steel, Bethlehem Steel, Inland Steel, Crucible Steel, or any other steel company; this land does not belong to Anaconda, Kennecott, Alcoa, or any other nonferous metal company; this land does not belong to any soulless corporation!

This land does not belong to the ICC, FPC, FCC, AEC, TVA, FDA, USDA, BLM, Forest Service, Fish and Wildlife Service, or any other federal or state alphabet agency!

This land does not belong to the president of the United States, the Congress of the United States, the governor of any state, or the legislatures of the fifty states. This land belongs to its people. This land belongs to you and this land belongs to me.

Don't just sit there like lambs waiting for the slaughter, or canaries waiting to see if the mine shaft is really safe. Don't just sit around talking about the environmental crisis, or worse yet, just listening to others talk about it.

Don't just sit there and bitch. Sue somebody!

VICTOR YANNACONE, a partner of Yannacone & Yannacone, represents the environmental section of the American Trial Lawyers Association.

PART IX

PEOPLE

That's the first thing to do—start controlling population in affluent white America, where a child born to a white American will use about fifty times the resources of a child born in the black ghetto.

—DAVID BROWER
Antioch College
Yellow Springs, Ohio
April 19

BOB PACKWOOD

Stop at Two

American University, Washington, D.C., April 22

We read and hear a great deal about the population problems of the rest of the world. We are told of impending famine in India. We are treated to daily reports of Latin American countries doubling their populations in fifteen to twenty years. It's frustrating that we may not be able to do much about the rest of the world. But it's a certainty that we'll never be able to do anything about the rest of the world unless we first restrain and stabilize our own population growth.

The United States now has slightly over 200 million people. Census projections indicate that even at our relatively low 1-percent-per-year current rate of increase, we'll have 300 million people within thirty years, and half a billion within seventy to eighty years. I would consider it a mark of progress if we achieve a zero population growth rate—if there are no more people in this country ten years from now than there are today.

The problem is not *feeding* half a billion people. Half a billion people can be fed, if we don't care about over-utilizing our croplands, and if we don't care about the ecological effects of doubling the use of agricultural pesticides for crops to feed twice as many people. Nor will housing be a problem. We can house half a billion people if we are willing to cut down all the trees in our national forests and then turn to—and eventually deplete—whatever wood substitute we might find. And we can probably even handle the air and water pollution and the solid waste produced by half a billion people.

But there is more to life than adequate food and decent housing, which, incidentally, we don't even provide for all our people now. There is more to life than just existing. If life is to have any meaning, then environmental quality must be preserved. On our current course, whatever environmental quality we have now will surely be destroyed in just providing subsistence for our additional millions.

I've spoken in most of the large towns of this country. I've yet to see any large town that was a better place to live simply because it had more industry or a richer tax base. I've yet to see any large town that had better schools or more parks or less noise or less air pollution simply because it's big. As a rule of thumb, the bigger a city gets, the less livable it is. . . .

Half a billion people in seventy years may seem unavoidable, but we are still masters of our own fate. The population explosion can be restrained, I think, if we right now take three important steps toward establishing a national population policy.

First, we must make family planning information and services available to *all* women regardless of their financial resources. A small step in this direction is S. 2108, which I have cosponsored. Our developmental research programs must be expanded and intensified so that several safe and effective contraceptives are available to meet the needs and preferences of all women. With 100 percent availability of contraceptives, no woman will become pregnant simply from lack of information about, or access to, adequate contraceptive devices.

The second necessary step is elimination of legal restrictions on abortion in this country. Abortion should be a matter of private conscience for every woman in this country. Whether or not she wishes to terminate an unwanted pregnancy should be a decision that solely she and her physician make. Dr. Charles F. Westoff of the Office of Population Research at Princeton University indicates that approximately 22 percent of the pregnancies among married couple in this country are unwanted by at least one spouse. There is no reason why a woman should be forced to continue an unwanted pregnancy. Once abortion is legalized, we must make certain that, as with contraceptive information, no woman is denied access merely for lack of financial resources.

The third step toward a zero population growth rate in the United States is a government taxation policy which encourages smaller families. Tax incentives are used to encourage oil exploration; to encourage the installation of pollution abatement devices; to foster the growth of pension plans. Why should we not use the tax incentive to tackle the most critical domestic problem in our country—the population crisis?

So far, I've had no great success in getting cosponsors on either the abortion bill or the tax deduction bill. . . . With your participation and your elected leaders' leadership, we'll succeed. . . . I'm tired of being slapped on the back and told what courage it took to introduce these bills, and that Senator X would love to support me, but . . . and then there are half a dozen different clauses that finish that sentence, all of which say—I won't support the bills now. . . . It is important that future generations look back and appreciate the sensible policies which we have implemented to achieve a stabilized population.

If they can breathe clean air and enjoy pure water . . . if they can still relish a cascading river tumbling through a deep gorge that has not been dammed because of the necessity to produce electric power . . . if they can walk through a forest that has not been completely cut to produce homes for half a billion people . . . and if they can find a place where tranquility and quiet are still an actuality, rather than a memory . . . then we will have fulfilled the adage which says:

> What we have in this life
> When we die will pass to somebody else;
> What we are in this life
> Will be ours forever.

SENATOR PACKWOOD is a Republican from Oregon.

THEODORE FOIN, JR.

STRANGERS

University of California, Davis, Calif., April 22

. . . Population density has one potentially important effect. Evidence is accumulating that we don't care very much for one another anymore, that we are more and more calling many more people "strangers." Studies on rats show physical and psychological changes that are attributable to the process of crowding. These include cannibalism, failure to care for young, overaggressive defense of territory, changes in the adrenal glands and in the liver, hyperactive nerves, highly irregular reproductive activity, and finally, premature death. Social scientists are finding that Americans are beginning to show signs of increasing isolation from one another. The result is increasing dehumanization—particularly in the large urban centers where people have become so conditioned to human suffering that they can successfully ignore it. . . .

THEODORE FOIN is an associate research systems ecologist at the University of California, Davis, Calif.

EUGENE P. ODUM

Five Acres

University of Georgia, Athens, Ga., April 22

The most important single problem faced by the human race is controlling and managing our own population on an optimum rather than a maximum basis. The population density that is optimum for the individual's welfare and freedom of action is much less than the maximum number of people that might be merely fed, housed and clothed as dehumanized robots or "domestic animals." Individual freedom can not be maintained and social problems can not possibly be solved under conditions of overpopulation. It is important to realize that the optimum population density for a highly technical and affluent society is very much lower than for a subsistence society because the individual's use of resources and his production of wastes is so much greater. Thus, the U. S. is now in as much danger of overpopulation at its level of living as is India at its level of living standards. We can not just sit back and let the food supply determine how many people the earth can support, because it will support more "warm bodies" than quality human beings.

To maintain an American diet and an American style of life, each person may need as many as five acres. Only a very small part of this five acres is needed to supply food, clothing and shelter, if we would be satisfied merely with getting enough calories, having one suit per year and living in a one-room apartment. But to support us in the good life to which we are accustomed, a lot of space is needed to take care of resource demands, domestic animals and recreation, and to cope with air, water, noise and other pollution.

Consider for the moment that one person in five acres

is a reasonable density. Georgia is rapidly approaching that level. . . . Georgia could be badly overpopulated by the year 2001!

EUGENE ODUM, professor of zoology and director of the Institute of Ecology of the University of Georgia, is the author of *Fundamentals of Ecology*.

RENE DUBOS

TEXTURES OF LIFE

Du Page University, April 22

. . . The population of the United States is increasing at a rate of approximately 1 percent a year. In contrast, the production of electric energy and the accumulation of wastes are increasing at the rate of 9 percent a year—which means that they will double in less than eight years. In view of these facts, environmental degradation and loss in the quality of life will continue to accelerate very rapidly in the United States even if we succeed in achieving zero population growth. The impact of technology therefore constitutes a more immediate threat than the population bomb and far more destructive because many of its effects will be irreversible. . . .

The ecological constraints on population and technological growth will inevitably lead to social and economic systems different from the ones in which we live today. In fact, all this was foreseen more than a century ago by John Stuart Mill who coined then the phrase "stationary state," to denote a stage of western civilization in which further *quantitative* growth would no longer be possible. Even though events will certainly validate John Stuart Mill's conclusions, the adjective "stationary" that he uses to define the forthcoming phase is unfortunate, because it seems to imply a complete end to change. The phrase "steady state" is more compatible with a dynamic equilibrium and continued *qualitative* change.

The "steady state" formula is so different from the philosophy of endless quantitative growth which has governed western civilization during the nineteenth and twentieth centuries that it may cause public alarm. Many persons will mistakenly assume that the world is entering a period of stagnation, leading eventually to decadence. Yet, a steady state can be favorable to creative changes. In fact, change within a closed system will probably offer intellectual possibilities much more challenging than those offered by the kind of rampant growth that prevails at present. . . .

The mounting roster of environmental threats has now become an obsession for the general public. And as a result, the technological utopians are almost silenced by the prophets of doom who publicize the dangers inherent in the population bomb; the exhaustion of natural resources; the pollution of air, water, and food; the massive poisoning of all ecological systems by pesticides and other toxic chemicals; the threat to oxygen production by toxic effects of pollutants on plankton; the possibility that the polar ice cap will melt and thus drown our cities because of the greenhouse effect, or that we are about to enter a new ice age because atmospheric pollutants will prevent the solar heat from reaching the Earth.

The biologists, ecologists, demographers, and students of natural resources who affirm that scientific technology is dragging the whole world on a course of self-destruction are now shaping the public mood of the 1970s. They provide an impressive documentation to justify their thesis that the year 2000 will see not the emergence of a technological utopia, but rather the progressive destruction of all forms of life. . . . And it is true indeed that we are progressively becoming tolerant of worse and worse environmental conditions, as we conform to the dictates of technology. But it is equally true that conditions not sufficiently dangerous to destroy life eventually ruin its quality.

While I reject completely the blind euphoric attitude of the technological utopians and share the preoccupations of the prophets of ecologic doom, I doubt that human life or other forms of life will be destroyed, except of course in the event of nuclear warfare. All living things exhibit an enormous degree of resilience. Mosquitoes become resistant to pesticides and algae grow luxuriously in waters massively contaminated with DDT. Similarly, man can survive and multiply under horrible conditions, despite shortages of food and amidst pollutants.

Ecological systems can develop tolerance to pollutants but in the process they tend to lose their rich complexity and stability. Technological accidents do not destroy all of life, but create undesirable conditions. . . . Social adaptability can have disastrous effects in the long run. Tolerance to pollution, crowding, noise, etc., must usually be paid for at a later date in the form of physical and mental misery.

René Dubos is a bacteriologist at Rockefeller University in New York City, an author, and a Pulitzer Prizewinner.

PART X

VIVA!

There is no confusion. It is planned. Subversive elements plan to make American children live in an environment that is good for them.

—Mrs. Samuel M. Neill
Daughters of the American Revolution
Constitution Hall
Washington, D.C.
April 22

JOHN V. LINDSAY

Do or Die

Pratt Institute, Brooklyn, N.Y., April 22

. . . We cannot escape the Earth we have made. Soon, we may reach the butt ends of our days and ways—smog, foul water, the claustrophobia of overcrowding, and noise so persistent and so loud you cannot hear yourself going quietly insane. What we really face is not air or water pollution, but the pollution of life itself. What is threatened is not merely the environment, but our senses and our reason.

This Earth Day testifies to the sudden, total realization that we have poisoned both the atmosphere and the inner air of tranquillity on which so much of the good life depends. In every part of America today, voices that have never been raised in protest have joined with voices worn by dissent to demand that we reclaim our Earth for its people. We must end this self-poison before it ends us. . . .

Most federal research funds are now pouring into the technology of death—into finding more sophisticated ways to kill in a world we can already annihilate a hundred times over. Just two days ago, the administration talked of vast expansions in our strategic weapons systems—when what we really need is a vast expansion in the peaceful tools of environmental reconstruction. We must find out how to clean up our rivers—how to dissipate the smog—how to dispose of garbage by compaction, not burning.

It will cost money. You do not defeat pollution with pronouncements. A national war on pollution that costs less than a squadrom of B-52s mocks its own purpose. A national war on pollution that hands the bill over to the cities betrays the future. But that is what is happening. And, we are told, it is all we can afford to do.

We can afford more. But only when we choose to stop

spending $30 billion a year in Vietnam pretending we are right. . . .

Will Earth Day be the new moratorium? Will the massive outpouring of words and emotions today encounter the same frustration of inattention and indifference? Will we meet again in a year to renew our protest—and then quietly disband?

I wish I could say no. Today one can only answer: Not necessarily. But there is much that we can do—through institutions, in our neighborhoods, and as individuals—to have our environment. This is the essential meaning of Earth Day.

Earth Day proves that we can act together. We have formed a new partnership today—a partnership for self-preservation—and we must make that partnership permanent. . . .

As we go on, we must also remember that pollution is not our only problem. We must not succumb to those who hope that concern with the environment will turn us away from Vietnam or civil rights. Pure water will not wash away the stain of an immoral war. And clean air will not dispel the odor of a society that tells only the poorest among us to ask what they can do for their country.

JOHN LINDSAY is the mayor of New York City.

GEORGE WILEY

Ecology and the Poor

Harvard University, Cambridge, Mass., April 21

. . . I want to speak to you tonight as a person who is black, and as a person who has been actively involved in organizing poor people for social and economic justice in this country over the last several years. I'd like to share with you some concerns that I have about the movement around environment and ecology.

My first question, as I observe you in your enthusiasm in this new movement, is whether this is a serious movement, or whether it is a passing fad that is simply a way for some people to cop out from dealing with some of the fundamental and pressing social problems that beset a lot of us in the society; whether it is something that will be approached and dealt with in an unrealistic way; whether you'll allow yourselves to be bought off by the proponents of the mass media who will infiltrate and take over your movement and brainwash you into dealing with problems that are trivial or irrelevant under the guise of a revolution in dealing with ecology. Or whether you are prepared to come to grips with some of the basic problems which we have in our society.

I would say that if you are a serious movement you must be prepared to take on the giant corporations who are the primary polluters and perpetrators of some of the worst conditions that affect the environment of the country and indeed the world. You must be prepared to develop substantial political power to confront those corporations, and to press for programs of massive government spending and programs involving substantial government control over the operations of those corporations, and indeed, I believe over the operations of many of the ways in which we go about our daily lives.

I think you have to be prepared for changes in the life-style and the mode of consumption to which most of you have become accustomed. Indeed, one of the most serious questions is whether you are prepared to deal with the problems that you have created yourselves, and to look at the nature of the society that this country has produced. . . .

For a substantial number of people to approach this problem in a half-serious way is going to do grave injury to black people and to poor people in this country and throughout the world. I say this with some consideration. I say this with some knowledge and experience, not only in seeing how other movements and other programs have dealt with poor people and black people, but specifically looking at some of the possible consequences of what your movement can do to poor people in this country.

Are you going to ask the poor people in this country to bear the cost of cleaning up air pollution and doing something about other environmental problems? In all likelihood a good many of the approaches that you are likely to take are going to be paid for directly at the expense of the poorest people in this country.

This will happen in a number of ways. It will happen, for example, because most of the systems of controlling air and water pollution, if they are imposed, will simply be passed along to the consumer in higher costs. The poor people, the people at the bottom of the economic ladder, will essentially be given a regressive tax—they will be asked to pay the same price you pay in terms of higher costs for such basic things as electric power, heat for homes, and other commodities essential to life itself. Unless some serious planning is done, it is going to be the poor people who pay for those things you do.

I'd like to cite an example in the state of Colorado. Some people got together with good intentions and got some air pollution ordinances, both in the state and in some of the cities. The result of that was that people could no longer burn their trash. A desirable thing—to stop polluting the atmosphere with smoke. Perhaps it could be argued that this is a minor source. But nonetheless, it is the kind of victory that the air pollution people are capable of winning, because you can't beat Con Edison; you can't beat some of the big companies. You go after some of the little ones that are beatable.

When this ordinance went into effect, the poor neighborhood became more polluted. People could not afford to have their trash taken to the dump, and there was no city trash-removal program. The people on welfare couldn't afford a car to get their trash to the dump. So people had to bear a cost they couldn't afford to remove their trash—which some did, but others simply didn't do it, and their neighborhoods became dirtier and more rodent-infested. In short, their environment further deteriorated as a direct result of something that was done in the other parts of the community. . . .

It has been my experience that most of you aren't going to deal with the problem at the level that it is going to help the welfare recipient, the poor person in the ghettos and the barrios. Most of you are not even going to listen to the voices coming from those communities. You won't ask what they want, and how they want to deal with the problems of their environment, or indeed whether they want to deal with the problems of environment at all—because they feel there are other more pressing priorities in their lives.

So far, to be invited to participate in a program on environment is the exception rather than the rule for poor people or black community organizations. In some cases already poor people's efforts to participate in programs on ecology have been rebuffed.

Is the ecology movement planning to place any serious priority on the problems of environment of the ghetto and the barrio, of our urban areas, where pollution is worse?

You must not embark on programs to curb economic growth without placing a priority on maintaining income, so that the poorest people won't simply be further depressed in their condition but will have a share, and be able to live decently.

Those of us who have studied the problem of jobs and income know that you are not going to be able to create enough jobs. If poor people, and particularly the blacks and other minorities, are not going to be left behind, and further exploited, it is going to be absolutely essential to the ecology movement that there be a national program guaranteeing a minimum adequate income for every citizen. . . .

It is going to be necessary to have substantial government expenditures for the programs of environmental control or, indeed, of industrial control. That means that you will be directly competing with poor people for very scarce government dollars. And if you are not in a position to mount a confrontation with the military-industrial complex, if you are not prepared to join with poor people in saying that this war in Vietnam has got to end, that we've got to stop U. S. military imperialism around the world, we've got to cut out the vast and wasteful military expenditures; if you are not prepared to say that we want to put a priority on dealing with urban environmental problems; if you are not prepared to put yourselves and your movement and your organization on the line for those things—quite clearly poor people will pay the cost of your ecology program. . . .

You must take into account the problem that most of the world is poor, and most of the world is colored, and most of the world is suspicious and distrustful of the rampant racism that exists in the United States. And if you are to develop strategies to control world population, and to deal with all of the myriad problems of the environment, you are going to have to recognize that you must deal initially with the problem of racism in the United States of America. . . .

It is going to be necessary to develop a politically sophisticated movement prepared to confront the military-industrial capitalist complex in the U. S. A. and prepared to develop a society based on human needs rather than a profit motive.

George Wiley is director of the National Welfare Rights Organization.

I. F. STONE

Con Games

Sylvan Theater, Washington, D.C., April 22

In the ancient world, the Caesars did it with bread and circuses. And tonight, I'm afraid, is the first time that our Caesars have learned to do it with rock and roll, and idealism, and noninflammatory social issues. In some ways, I'm sorry to say, we here tonight are being conned. This has many of the aspects of a beautiful snow job. The country is slipping into a wider war in southeast Asia, and we're talking about litterbugs. The secretary of defense, on Monday, made a speech to the Associated Press sabotaging the SALT talks, presenting a completely false picture of the world balance of power, ending what little hope we had of progress in those talks, preparing the way for a bigger, more expensive arms race at the expense of mankind, and we're talking as if we needed more wastebaskets.

The divisions of white and black in this country are getting to the point where they threaten our future, and we're talking about pollution. And it's not that pollution is not an important subject, but if the Nixon administration feels so deeply about it, why don't they do something substantial about it?

One important thing about this town is that you can never take very seriously what the officials say. They're the prisoners of a vast bureaucracy. Much of what they say is merely a rationalization of their lack of momentum. But in particular, the president said, and I think quite rightfully and quite truthfully, that in the next ten years it's now or never for the air we breathe and the water we drink. And then, after making that speech, he put in a budget in which 52 cents out of every general revenue dollar goes to the military, and barely four-tenths of one cent goes to air and water pollution. And that's a real con game. And that's a real snow job.

We are spending, on new weapons systems alone, more than ten times as much, in this coming fiscal year, in the Nixon budget, than we're going to spend on air and water. We're spending a billion dollars more a year on space than all our expenditure on natural resources. The priorities of this government are lunatic—absolutely lunatic. And we're not going to save the air we breathe and the water we drink without very many fundamental changes in governmental policy and governmental structure.

Before I came down here tonight, I heard a TV announcer say with great satisfaction that he hadn't heard a word said about Vietnam all day. Well, I'm going to say a word about Vietnam. We're not going to be able to save our air and our water, and the resources of our country, for our children and our grandchildren, until we end the militarization of our society, until we bring to an end the effort of American imperialism to rule the world and to waste our resources and our honor and our kids on a futile and murderous and insane task.

The problem of pollution is not going to be solved in isolation. The basic and most important pollution problem that we have to deal with is to prevent the pollution of the atmosphere of free discussion by the Nixon-Agnew-Mitchell administration. A society can only progress and deal with its evils if it is prepared to allow the widest measure of free speech, including free speech for radicals who are completely opposed to the basis of that society. Any society allows you to agree with the government. A free society allows you to disagree fundamentally. And it takes a lot of disagreement, and a lot of hollering and a lot of demonstration, to shake any establishment out of its accustomed ways. And the main menace to the solution of these problems is an administration that thinks they will go away if they just put a few radicals in jail.

The problems are enormous. The source of pollution is man. And man's technology. And the enormous institutions he has built up that make him a prisoner. And somehow we've got to shake loose. And the biggest menace—the institution that ties us down most—that wastes our substance—that threatens to waste more of our youth—is that great big, five-sided building across the Potomac—

the Pentagon. They are preparing to do to us at home what they tried to do in Vietnam.

Only this week, General Wheeler, the retiring chairman of the joint chiefs of staff, gave an interview to *U.S. News and World Report* in which he said that criticism of the military was due to a Communist plot. This is an effort of the military to revive McCarthyism, to preserve its enormous power and privileges in our society. And until its power is broken, until the military is reduced sharply in size, we're not going to be able to solve these problems.

You know, there is no use talking about Earth Day unless we are prepared to make these fundamental changes. Everybody's talking about Earth Day, and it comes out of the mouths of so many hypocrites it turns your stomach. What kind of an Earth Day can we celebrate in a country that is spending so much of its money to destroy the Earth? How can we talk of reverence for life when we're spending so much on our enemy, our genius, our money, and our youth on building up new means of destroying life?

What's the use of talking about the pollution of air and water when we live under a precarious balance of terror which can, in an hour's time, make the entire Northern Hemisphere of our planet unlivable? There's no use talking about Earth Day until we begin to think like Earthmen. Not as Americans and Russians, not as blacks and whites, not as Jews and Arabs, but as fellow travelers on a tiny planet in an infinite universe. All that we can muster of kindness, of compassion, of patience, of thoughtfulness, is necessary if this tiny planet of ours is not to go down to destruction. Until we have a leadership willing to make the enormous changes—psychological, military, and bureaucratic—to end the existing world system, a system of hatred, of anarchy, of murder, of war and pollution, there is no use talking about buying more wastebaskets or spending a couple of hundred million dollars on the Missouri River. If we do not challenge these fundamental causes of peril, we will be conned by the establishment while basic decisions are being made over which we have very little control, though they endanger everything on which our future and the world's depend.

I. F. STONE is the editor and publisher of *I. F. Stone's Bi-Weekly.*

EDWARD M. KENNEDY

ON VIOLENCE

Yale Political Union, New Haven, Conn., April 22

Blacks interrupted Senator Kennedy's speech at Yale, demanding that the university contribute a half million dollars to the legal defense of the Black Panthers charged in New Haven with murder and kidnapping. Kennedy departed from his prepared address.

I cannot presume to speak for Yale on these demands, but I will say on the subject of violence that under no conditions should violence be accepted and under no conditions should violence be employed.

I do not believe that violence brings change. I think violence brings self-indulgence and in the end violence can only bring repression and reaction. It will make law and order, rather than justice and the quality of life, the overriding political concerns of our times.

I can say, unfortunately, that I am an authority on violence, and it always brings pain and suffering [here the senator's voice broke] and there's no place for that in our society.

* * *

There are some who criticize our newfound concern over the environment. They charge that students and other Americans are turning their backs on other major issues confronting the United States, and are engaging in an "ecological cop-out." I do not share this view. But, as I look at the state of our national affairs today, I see the need to arm ourselves against this possibility. . . .

If war is unhealthy for children and other living things then the war belongs on the agenda of Earth Day.

What difference does it make that 150,000 young people will be home next spring if any year 5,000 to 8,000 more young men may die?

What in the world does Vietnamization mean to the 150,000 Vietnamese civilians—women, children, and old men—who will be casualties by next April? . . . You have not in the past, and you will not now, adopt one worthy cause at the expense of all the others. I remember how Martin Luther King responded when he was criticized for protesting against the Vietnam war instead of confining himself to the area of civil rights. "I have fought segregation too long," he said, "for me to segregate my moral concerns."

None of us can segregate our moral concerns. We cannot fight air pollution in New York and ignore the oppressive environment of Harlem. We cannot ban 2, 4, 5-T in the United States and ignore the use of napalm in Vietnam. We cannot forget that for millions of poor Americans, the desire for a better environment does not mean open spaces or country air or swimmable rivers. For these millions—in areas of urban and rural poverty—the real threats of the environment are still the ancient evils of ignorance, crime, and disease. . . .

Particularly on this day, when we are gathered to celebrate life, let us not reject the avenues of peaceful change. Let us dedicate ourselves to remaking our environment in the broadest sense, to ensuring that a beautiful America is also a just and compassionate America.

SENATOR KENNEDY is a Democrat from Massachusetts.

MARGARET MEAD

EARTH PEOPLE

Bryant Park, New York City, April 22

. . . The relationship to a primary environment and the view of that environment is something about which we know quite a few things. We know, for instance, that the Swedes were willing to travel all the way to Minnesota to live in the same kind of country rather than move from the country to the city. We know that Sicilians and southern Italians moved to south Jersey to find land for their vineyards like the land they had before. We have a good many studies of refugees who have found themselves extraordinarily disoriented in another country where there was no water, when they were used to water, or where there were no mountains, and they were used to mountains. . . .

It's exceedingly important how people feel about their environment, whether they feel that it's something that's friendly, or something that's hostile. Colin Turnbull, in the delightful book *The Forest People,* has given a vivid description of the way the pygmies feel that they belong to the forest and the forest cares for them. The whole of life is thought of as a relationship to this great forest, whom they mustn't offend and who will look after them. . . .

When we deal with children growing up in America . . . we find some who are trying to escape from everything that the modern environment stands for, who think of our contemporary environment as an amalgam of cities that are falling to pieces, of pollution that is choking us, of living that are dying, of people who are being starved, and of people who are being killed. They go off and try to found communes where they will be closer to the earth. . . .

We have had a tremendous amount of discussion that

echoes and re-echoes in the minds of young people as they're growing up, as to whether technology is a monster and we should get rid of it, and whether man has committed the unforgivable sin—the sin of having separated himself from the environment and from other men, of having separated himself from himself. We hear discussions going on everywhere as to whether there is a possible new religious phrasing of the relationship to the environment. . . .

Young people have a sense of this planet that older people did not have when they grew up. They have a sense of the unity of the human race that older people had only as a dream. . . .

All of these things are linked together—our feeling about the whole planet, our feeling about war, our feeling about population, our recognition that the population must now be balanced in relation to the earth, our feeling about the environment.

If we put all of these things together into a new ethic, that ethic ought to give us the possibility of inventing the kind of scientific advances and technological advances which will cope successfully with what we're doing.

In the past, the individual pollution, what's happened to this lake, what was done by this factory, what was done in this city, what was done by this country and that country, have all been fragmentary dangers. They've been fragmentary pieces of behavior by people who couldn't see all of it.

We have today the knowledge and the tools to look at the whole earth, to look at everybody on it, to look at its resources, to look at the state of our technology, and to begin to deal with the whole problem. I think that the tenderness that lies in seeing the earth as small and lonely and blue is probably one of the most valuable things that we have now. . . .

MARGARET MEAD is an anthropologist and author.

ARTURO SANDOVAL

LA RAZA

Albuquerque, N.M., April 22

There are two things we want to talk about today. One of them is what has happened to this country. And the other is what we hope will happen. I think all of us have realized that, having gone through the educational system in this country, and being different—most of us having spoken Spanish when we started—we understand what has happened to this counrty. We know that there is a fear among people. People are afraid of their humanity because systematically they have been taught to become inhuman. They have no understanding, they have no appreciation, of people who are different.

They have no understanding of what it is to love nature. And so our airs are being polluted, our rivers are being poisoned, and our land is being cut up. . . . They have no understanding that our father is the sun and our mother is the Earth. And that is sad, more than anything else.

There can be no hate, there can be no violence directed against these people. We have to understand that these people sit on the boards of directors of large corporations. They have been taught the morality of profit making. They have been taught that money is God, and that is all. And I think that most of us in the audience today realize that the symbols of this society are dying. We have come to realize that the humanity in all of us is being oppressed and destroyed by the very systems that we created to try to help us to make life a little easier—to make it a little better.

So what do we have left? And what do we do, and what do we hope for. We are gathered here today next to a sewage plant in Albuquerque to say "Viva la raza." And I want to talk about that concept, "la raza."

"La raza"—"the race"—goes beyond surname and goes beyond skin color. And it doesn't address itself only to those of us who call ourselves "Chicano." And it doesn't talk about only those people who have suffered. But it talks about all those people who have an understanding of their humanity. And who wish to share that humanity with others. That is what we hope—and that is what we hope April 22, Earth Day, will be. . . . We hope to give of that humanity and humanize the technology that we have created—humanize it so that we can reap its benefits, and be able to control how it is used to help all our brothers in the Third World and all people in the universe.

So today is, basically, a very hopeful day—a beginning. A day that says that we can bring our brothers down—those people who live in $40,000 homes—can bring them together and touch their humanity and teach them what it is. That is what "la raza" addresses itself to. We talk about reaching people and touching them and teaching them what their humanity is. And when we say "Viva la raza" we command "la raza" to live, because humanity is dying. And America—white America—has lost its ability to cry, and laugh and sing and love and live. And that is what we are addressing here today. Our humanity, our hope, and our determination to make this society—and all societies—human societies, livable societies. And to make those environments human, life-supporting kinds of environments. So I close by saying, "Viva la raza."

ARTURO SANDOVAL is western coordinator for Environmental Action.

MARYA MANNES

HYMN OF THANKSGIVING

Bryant Park, New York City, April 22

This is a hymn of thanksgiving from the people of the United States to their gods: the god of plenty, the god of profit, and the goddess of convenience:

Lords of Affluence and Avarice, Holy Creators of the Gross National Product, accept herewith these sacrifices in gratitude for the American continent which you bestowed on us, with all its mountains, rivers, lakes, seas, and valleys, and with the liberty given to each of us to do with them what we pleased.

In boundless gratitude for all this wealth, O gods of plenty, profit, and convenience, we lay at your feet a hundred billion cans of beer and bottles of Coke, sixty billion plastic containers and paper wrappings, ninety billion tons of raw sewage, and enough lethal chemicals in air and water to kill legions of animals and to invade our lungs with deadly gases and our blood with deadly poisons.

O lords of affluence and avarice, we repay this infinite generosity of the Gross National Product with Gross National Pollution: seas of oil, rivers of cars, the ugliest cities in the world, and all the sick and poor and criminal human waste produced by them.

These we have made in your name from the boundless beauties you stole from the Creator of all living things. May we now expiate these massive crimes by repudiating you and by restoring the beauty of life on Earth before its death claims us all.

Amen.

MARYA MANNES is a writer and critic.

Appendix

It is impossible to live an ecologically sound life in the United States. Industry has the advantage of lobbyists in government and advertising everywhere. The individual citizen can do little.

But it is possible for groups, organized at the local level, to be effective. They can pressure government agencies to do their jobs, and they can begin to make corporations act responsibly. Among other things, they can bring suits, demonstrate, boycott, and support candidates who will bridge the gap between rhetoric and action.

The following are regional groups active in the fight to save the environment. For further information, write Environmental Action, 2000 P Street, N.W., Washington, D.C. 20036.

CALIFORNIA

Berkeley:

Ecology Action
Cliff Humphrey
P.O. Box 9334
Berkeley, Calif. 94709
(415) 848-3388

Los Angeles:

World Life Day: June 22
Richard Register
Robin Cranston
World Life Day
P.O. Box 69683
Los Angeles, Calif. 90069

San Francisco:

Student Environmental Confederation
1650 Jones St.
San Francisco, Calif. 94109

CONNECTICUT

New Haven:

Yale Environmental Action
550 Osborn Laboratory
Yale University
New Haven, Conn. 06520

ILLINOIS

Champaign:

Students for Environmental Controls
c/o YMCA
1001 S. Wright Ave.
University of Illinois
Champaign, Ill. 61820

Chicago:

Campaign Against Pollution
65 E. Huron St.
Chicago, Ill. 60611

Chicago Earth Force Committee
109 N. Dearborn
Chicago, Ill. 60602

IOWA

Iowa City:

LIFE
University of Iowa
Iowa City, Iowa 52240

KANSAS

Wichita:

Association for Environmental Improvement
Box 26
Wichita State University
Wichita, Kansas 67208

MAINE

Orono:

The Effluent Society
General Student Senate
42 Lord Hall
University of Maine
Orono, Me. 04473

Portland:

Southern Maine Environmental Action Committee
68 High St.
Portland, Me. 04101

MASSACHUSETTS

Amherst:

Environmental Action
c/o King Council
207 Hampshire House
University of Massachusetts
Amherst, Mass. 01002

Cambridge:
Ecology Action Center
925 Massachusetts Ave.
Cambridge, Mass. 02139

MICHIGAN

Ann Arbor:
ENACT
School of Natural Resources
University of Michigan
Ann Arbor, Mich. 48104

Rochester:
PLEA
Student Activities
Oakland University
Rochester, Mich. 48063

MINNESOTA

Minneapolis:
Environmental Action
% Koffman Memorial Union
University of Minnesota
Minneapolis, Minn. 55455

MISSOURI

St. Louis:
Black Survival
% Union Sarah Gateway Center
4957 Delmar Blvd.
St. Louis, Mo. 63108

Coalition for the Environment
Rm. 706, Security Bldg.
319 N. 4th St.
St. Louis, Mo. 63102

NEBRASKA

Lincoln:
Citizens for Environmental Improvement
333 N. 14th St.
Lincoln, Nebraska 68508

NEW HAMPSHIRE

Durham:
UNHITE
Wolf House
8 Ballard St.
Durham, N.H. 03824

NEW YORK

Albany:
Protect Your Environment
State University of New York
Environmental Forum
Fine Arts 218
Albany, N.Y. 12203

New York City:
Environment!
119 5th Ave.
New York, N.Y. 10003

Environmental Action Coalition of New York City
235 E. 49th St.
New York, N.Y. 10017

NORTH DAKOTA

Grand Forks:
Students for Environmental Defense
% Biology Dept.
University of North Dakota
Grand Forks, N.D. 58201

OHIO

Ashtabula:
Citizens for Survival
Student Activities
Kent State University—Ashtabula Branch
Ashtabula, Ohio 44004

Cincinnati:
Ohio Students Environmental Council
% Mark Nagel, Chairman
3379 Rodeo Court
Cincinnati, Ohio 45211

OKLAHOMA

Oklahoma City:
ECCO
% Dept. of Human Ecology
School of Public Health
University of Oklahoma Medical School
Oklahoma City, Okla. 73104

OREGON

Portland:
Students for Oregon Environment
421 11th Ave., S.W.
Portland, Ore. 97205

RHODE ISLAND

Providence:
Ecology Action of Rhode Island
50 Olive St.
Providence, R.I. 02906

VERMONT

Burlington:
Committee for Environmental Action
Box 99 Billings Center
University of Vermont
Burlington, Vt. 05401

WASHINGTON

Seattle:
Project Survival—David Sucher
3130 Franklin E.
Seattle, Wash. 98102

WISCONSIN

Madison:
Ecology Students Association
% Dept. of Zoology
University of Wisconsin
Madison, Wis. 53706

Milwaukee:
M.U.S.T.B.E.
% John Hoak
841 N. 15th St.
Milwaukee, Wis. 53233

In addition, here are some consumer hints.

RECYCLING

Buy returnable bottles of milk, soft drinks, beer, etc. Return them.

Use cloth napkins, towels, tablecloths, place mats, handkerchiefs, diapers.

Use china dishes.

Use a nylon carrier for groceries rather than paper bags.

Carry a lunch box.

Store food in reusable containers.

Share magazine subscriptions.

Keep a blackboard (rather than paper) near the phone.

Return newspapers to paper companies, aluminum cans to aluminum companies for reuse.

Reuse gift wrappings, ribbons, etc.

Use junk mail for your children to drawn on.

Use vegetable scraps for compost piles.

CONSUMER

Transportation

Ride a bicycle. Walk. Jog.

Use public transportation.

Join a car pool.

Buy a four- or six-cylinder car.

Detergents

The following list compares phosphate percentages. The list was researched and compiled by Pollution Probe and the University of Toronto, Canada. The lower the percentage, the cleaner the product.

HEAVY DUTY LAUNDRY PRODUCTS

Product	Percent Phosphate	Manufacturer
Ivory Snow	1.0	Procter & Gamble
Lux	1.0	Lever Brothers
Instant Fels	9.0	Purex Corp.
Wisk	10.5	Lever Brothers
Amaze	27.0	Lever Brothers
Breeze	27.0	Lever Brothers
Surf	32.0	Lever Brothers
Bold	32.5	Procter & Gamble
Duz	35.0	Procter & Gamble
Omo	36.0	Lever Brothers
Ajax II	36.0	Colgate Palmolive
Fab	36.5	Colgate Palmolive
Amway SAB	36.5	Amway Corp.
All	39.0	Lever Brothers
Drive	41.5	Lever Brothers
Tide XK	43.5	Procter & Gamble
Oxydol	44.5	Procter & Gamble
Cheer	44.5	Procter & Gamble
Peri	47.0	Sep-Ko
Bio-Ad	49.0	Colgate Palmolive

LIGHT DUTY PRODUCTS

Product	Percent Phosphate	Manufacturer
Zero	7.5	Boyle Midway Co.
Dreft	34.0	Procter & Gamble

DISHWASHER COMPOUNDS

Product	Percent Phosphate	Manufacturer
Swish	29.0	Curley Corp.
Amway	34.0	Amway Corp.
Cascade	36.5	Procter & Gamble
Calgonite	42.0	Calgon
Finish	43.0	Economics
All	45.0	Lever Brothers

LIQUID DISHWASHING COMPOUNDS

All liquid dishwashing compounds that were tested were less than 1% phosphate.

MISCELLANEOUS

Product	Percent Phosphate	Product	Percent Phosphate
Pinesol	1.0	Mr. Clean	6.5
Dutch Bleach	1.0	Spic and Span	21.0
Downy	1.0	Snowy Bleach	22.0
Fleecy	1.0	Solvease	32.0
Arm and Hammer Sal Soda	1.0	Amway Water Softener	73.0
Ajax All Purpose	6.5	Calgon (water softener)	75.5

DDT

Wash and peel all fruits and vegetables.

Use flypaper and flyswatters to control insects (avoid "No-Pest Strips" made by Shell).

Plant a garden.

Avoid fertilizer with "arsenate" (arsenic) and chemical sprays.

ELECTRICITY

Turn off unnecessary lights.

Run your dishwasher only when full.

Use nonelectric toothbrushes, can openers, scissors, typewriters, frying pans, hair curlers, etc.

Dry clothes on a clothesline.